GW00707398

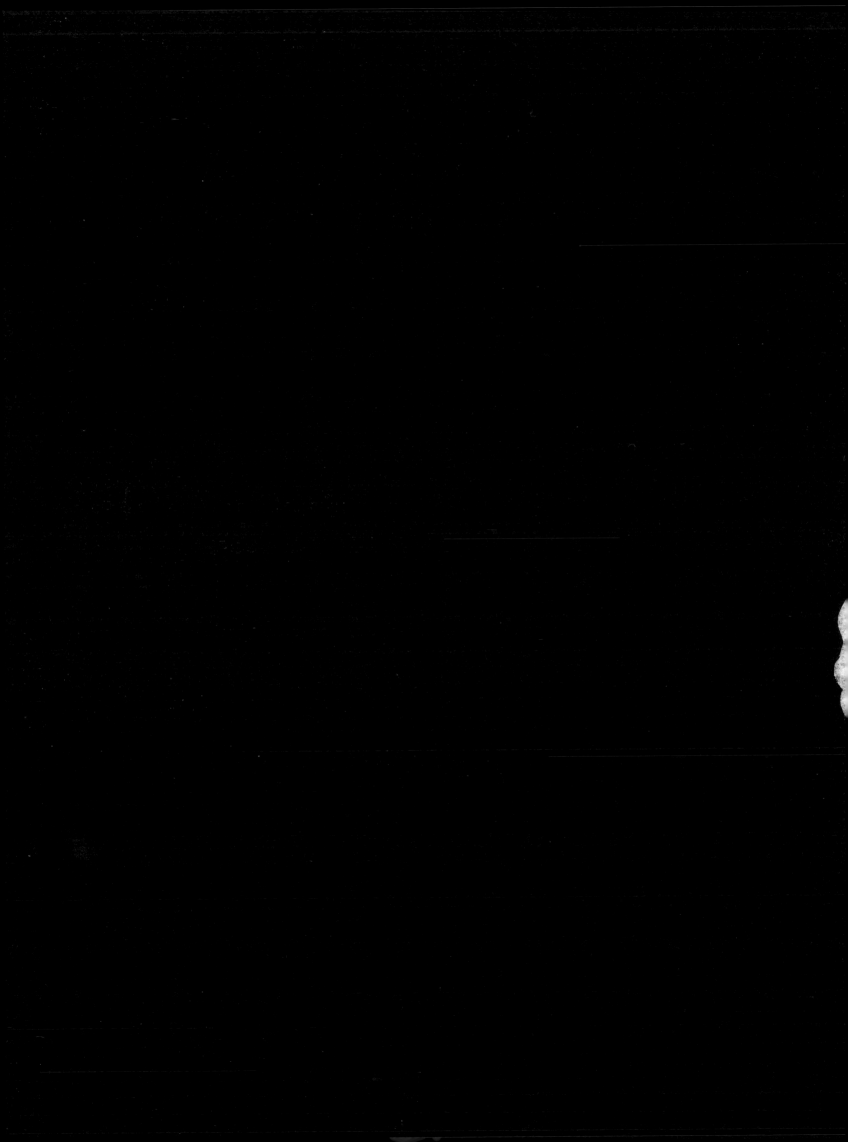

IVA BABAJA
*Icograda Vice President 2007-2011*

# Design as a potent agent of change

I had the privilege of observing the ED jury back in 2008 and recently in 2010. While the first thing that impressed me back in 2008 (and still does) was the extremely high and professional standard maintained by this unique jury, in 2010 my perspective has shifted together with the circumstances designers share all over the world. The overall crisis was expected to significantly lower the number of entries in all design competitions, and so it did in many cases, but the ED actually saw an increase in submissions. What this tells us is that even in times that call for heavy prioritizing, designers not only take pride and invest in their work being recognised with equal enthusiasm, but also that in selecting perhaps fewer places to seek that recognition they have chosen ED as the competition that will put their work in the most relevant perspective.

It is a great pleasure to see this young competition grow into maturity and become one of the most relevant places for honouring design accomplishments from all over Europe. The growth in both the number of entries and of countries that are included in ED is a definite proof that designers trust and hold it in high esteem. In its beginning it was a bold gesture, and perhaps even a gamble, to choose such a different concept of jury but it only goes to show that a visionary approach and thinking outside of the box yields wonderfully fruitful results. It also proves how much the communication design community has to gain by including other disciplines concerned with design into its family and how collaboration among them helps create a whole new level of quality and excellence.

# TABLE OF
# CONTENTS

**INTRODUCTION**          **JUDGING COMMITTEE**

**IDENTITY**

**DIGITAL MEDIA**

**PUBLICATIONS**

# TABLE OF CONTENTS

**ILLUSTRATIONS**

**SELF PROMOTION**

**PACKAGING**

**INDEX**

**SPECIAL PRIZES**

**VARIOUS**

## JACEK MROWCZYK
*(Poland)*

**Co-founder, editor of the graphic design section.**

Jacek Mrowczyk, born in Krakow in 1972. Graphic designer, graduated from the Academy of Fine Arts in Krakow in 1998 (Poland). Lecturer in the Department of Visual Communication at the AFA in Krakow (1999-2007). Awarded several prizes and special mentions (inter alia at the 18th International Biennial of Graphic Design in Brno, Czech Republic in 1998 and at the 16th Biennial of the Polish Poster in Katowice, Poland in 1999).

Co-founder and editor of a Polish design quarterly 2+3D. He received his Doctor of Art from the Academy of Fine Arts in Krakow in 2005. Jury member of national and international graphic design competitions. Author of several articles about design and a Polish Dictionary of Typographic Terms. Member of the Polish Graphic Design Association (STGU) and Association Typographique Internationale (ATypI). A Fulbright scholar at the Cooper-Hewitt National Design Museum in New York, USA (2001/2002) and a Kosciuszko Foundation scholar at the Rhode Island School of Design in Providence, USA (2006/2007).

Assistant professor at the Academy of Fine Arts in Katowice (Poland). Visiting teacher in the Rhode Island School of Design in Providence (USA).

## PETER BANKOV
*(Russia)*

**Editor in chief**

Peter Bankov was born in 1969. He graduated from Minsk Art College in 1988 and Moscow State Polygraph Institute in 1993.
1996 – he organized [kAk] magazine. Now it's one of the key points of graphic design creative progress by forming of energetic communicational space among its audience. Peter Bankov is "Design Depot" (www.designdepot.ru) founder and creator director.

Awards: Victoria National Award at the "Design" All-Russian exhibition-competition (1997, 1998, 2001), 1st diploma at the "Grahit" Moscow Festival (1998), Diploma of the Russian Union of Designers and Special prize of the "Design and Advertising" exhibition (1999), 2nd Award at the "Press Prize" Festival (2000), 1st Award (2003), 2nd Award (1999, 2001, 2003), 3rd Award (two times in 2002) at the Moscow International Festival Advertising, 1st Award (two times in 2004), 2nd Award (2004,2005), 3rd award (2004), Gold, Silver (2006) at the Kiev International Festival of Advertising , two Golden medals and Bronze medal (2005, 2008), Gold and Silver (2007) at the "ADCR Award" competition, 3rd Award at the Identity: Best Of The Best 2006; 3rd Awards at the Moscow International Festival Advertising Red Apple (2007, 2008), 1st Prize at ProdExpoPack 2007, 1st and 2nd Award at the XI Federal Competition of Annual Reports of RTS Stock Exchange (2008).

## ATHANASIOS KYRATZOGLOU
*(Greece)*

**Creative Director**

Graphic and Web Designer, born in Thessaloniki, Greece, now based in Athens. Creative Director of Tribal DDB Athens since 2007. With 10 years experience on design, he has worked for major newspapers and magazines, publications and clients in his country (Nike, Vodafone, Toyota, Axe, Unilever, Alpha Bank, Eleftherotypia etc.), winning awards on a national level. He writes for arts and design on various magazines and his personal blog. Freelancer on his own studio, since January 2010.

**2+3D grafika plus produkt**
www.2plus3d.pl

**[kAk]**
www.kak.ru

**+design**
www.designmag.gr

## MICHEL
## CHANAUD
*(France)*

**Editor & Art Director**

Leader and founder of the company Pyramyd which publishes the French magazine Étape: In 1989, Michel Chanaud launched the French magazine Étapes and Pyramyd Editions.

Formed in visual creation in the Ensad, he made his first weapons in interior architecture, scenography and design. He continued his career as a graphic designer freelance journalist especially for projects of packaging and in advertising creation. Before founding his publishing society, he started a graphic studio of creation.

During last years, he created a center of training in graphics. He also has extended the range of its publications, with the first magazine on the design of animation published, the DVD magazine DESIGNFLUX. Moreover, he is the editor of a hundred books on the design, like the collection D&D - design&designer – or like Émergence, a volume on young creation.

## MARTIN
## LENGAUER
*(Austria)*

**Head of Communication, designaustria**

Born in 1969. He studied philosophy, philology, political and communication science. Free lance journalist, founder and CEO of "die jungs kommunikation", a Vienna-based PR-agency. "die jungs" offer full service in public relations, text-production, media-conception and event-management for private, public, cultural, scientific and non-profit enterprises. Among them many design-related companies as well as the "designforum Vienna" and "designaustria", the umbrella organisation of Austrian designers, where Martin leads the communication department.

He also holds a teaching position in public relations at the University of Vienna. designaustria issues a quarterly, the "DA mitteilungen", which addresses all designaustria members as well as the Austrian design community.

## THIERRY
## HAUSERMANN
*(Switzerland)*

**Editor and Art Director**

Based in Morges/Lausanne, Switzerland, IDPURE magazine was founded by Thierry Hausermann in 2004. Dedicated to the provision of cutting edge, contemporary and personalized graphic design culture, Thierry emphasizes personal involvement in design and artistic projects like IDPURE. Thierry believes that graphic design should serve and support the needs of products or messages, which can only be achieved through up-close collaboration and understanding between clients and graphic/product designers, artists, etc. Thierry's motivation is to discover new talents and explore the possibilities of presenting them in IDPURE.

Thierry followed a one year program at ESAA (école supérieure d'arts appliqués) in Vevey, Switzerland, than studied a 4 year graphic design program at ERACOM (école romande d'arts et communication) in Lausanne, Switzerland, where he graduated in 1986. Thierry also pursued a course of studies at the Academy of Arts of San Francisco for 1 year in 1997. In addition to the graphic designer piece, he is an editor, a writer and a project manager.

**étapes**
www.etapes.com

**designaustria & DA mitteilungen**
www.designaustria.at

**idpure**
www.idpure.ch

## RUDOLF
## VAN WEZEL
*(The Netherlands)*

**Publisher**

Rudolf van Wezel (1956) studied publishing at the Frederik Muller Academy in Amsterdam and has worked in the Dutch Publishing industry since 1982.

Rudolf founded BIS Publishers in 1986. BIS is an international publisher in the field of graphic design, communication, product design, fashion and architecture. BIS publishes about 25 titles per year and most of them are in English and distributed all over the world. BIS has published Items Magazine, the Dutch national design magazine, for 15 years but sold this title to another Dutch publisher in 2007.

Rudolf also co-founded Frame Publishers and Mark Publishers. Frame is the international interior and design magazine that become a global player with a vast international distribution. Frame is now also available in licensed editions in Turkish, Russian and Chinese. Mark is the international Architectural magazine by the makers of Frame. Mark won the 2008 European Design Award for best magazine design. Rudolf started Graphic Magazine on international graphic visual culture in 2006. In the fall of 2009 Graphic will be revamped under a new name.

In 2008 Rudolf founded the Creative Company Conference which is an international yearly conference on creativity, innovation and entrepreneurship in Amsterdam.

**Elephan**
www.elephantmag.com
www.bispublishers.nl
www.framemag.com
www.mark-magazine.com
www.creativecompanyconference.com

## SILVIA
## SFLIGIOTTI
*(Italy)*

**Member of the editorial board**

Silvia Sfligiotti is a designer, educator and design writer based in Milano. She's a founding partner at Alizarina, a graphic and new media design studio. Silvia is co-author of three books on Italian graphic and type design; the most recent is Italic 2.0: contemporary type design in Italy (2008).

In 2008 she co-curated the Multiverso conference and exhibition during the Icograda Design Week Torino. She teaches typography and history of graphic design at the Scuola Politecnica di Design and is project leader for Visual Communication at the Faculty of Design and Art of the Free University of Bozen. She also lectured at international conferences and several Italian universities and design schools. Silvia is on the editorial board of «Progetto Grafico» since 2007, and she regularly contributes to the magazine; her articles were also published in other design magazines such as «Abitare», «Typo» and «Artlab».

**Progetto Grafico**
www.aiap.it/progettografico

## BETTINA
## SCHULZ
*(Germany)*

**Chief editor**

Bettina Schulz (born 1974 in Munich) has been editor-in-chief of the international journal novum World of Graphic Design since 2001. She joined the editorial staff of the magazine in 1994. Mrs Schulz also works as a freelance writer and editor for national and international magazines and for a range of clients in different sectors.

Bettina Schulz already serves on a number of design juries (e.g. for red dot communication design award, for the Best of Corporate Publishing Award, for the MfG competition of the Bundesverband Druck, Monaco de Luxe Packaging Award, Canon Pro Fashional Award, Adobe Photoshop Award, twice-yearly diploma awards presentation at the U5 Academy) and is co-founder of the »Creative Paper Conference« (www.creative-paper.de) in Munich.

**novum World of Graphic Design**
www.novumnet.de

## LINDA KUDRNOVSKÁ
*(Czech Republic)*

## BEATRIZ SAN ROMAN
*(Spain)*

## AYSE KONGUR
*(Turkey)*

**Editor-in-chief**

**Visual Magazine Editorial Director**

**International editor**

Linda Kudrnovská (born 1977) is a design writer and theoretician. She is the Editor-in-Chief and one of the founding members of TYPO, a Prague-based magazine focused on design and typography.Having studied graphic design and illustration, she graduated in theory of culture and history of art at the Faculty of Fine Arts, Charles University, Prague. Ever since, she has been a member of the editorial board of the TYPO Magazine; she also regularly contributes to a number of other periodicals.

Born in Barcelona, Spain, in 1969. Graduate in Information Sciences by the UCM, Madrid. Scriptwriter and theme installations designer. Journalist in Visual since 1990. Collaborates with different media as a free-lance writer.

Ayse Kongur studied graphic design at the Dokuz Eylül University Faculty of Fine Arts in Izmir. She worked at some of Turkey's leading branding and advertising agencies before relocating to the United Kingdom in 2006.

As international editor of Grafik Tasarim, Turkey's magazine of visual culture and communication, she writes critically on the arts and design and has conducted interviews with many of the world's leading designers.

She founded Kongur Design in 2008, providing branding solutions and creative services for internet-based and traditional companies.

**TYPO**
www.magtypo.cz

**Visual**
www.visual.gi

**Grafik Tasarim**
www.grafiktasarim.com.tr

## LYNDA
## RELPH-KNIGHT
*(UK)*

## FREEK
## KROESBERGEN
*(The Netherlands)*

endorsed by:

**Editor**

**Editor-in-chief**

Lynda Relph-Knight has been editor of
Design Week since 1989 and oversees the
weekly magazine, its supplements and
the website. Before taking up that role on
the world's only weekly design magazine,
she worked freelance, specialising in
the built environment and design.

In 2001 Lynda received an honorary MA
from the Surrey Institute of Art & Design
and is a fellow of the Royal Society of
Arts. She became an honorary fellow of
the Royal College of Art in June 2007.

Freek Kroesbergen (1972) is communications
manager of the Association of Dutch
Designers (BNO), and editor-in-chief of
design trade magazine Vormberichten,
which is published by BNO.

He studied marketing, communication and
concept development (strategy and copy
writing), and started his career in 1996 in the
advertising industry, working for international
agency Euro RSCG as information manager and
brand strategy planner. In 2003, he worked
in the same function for brand consultancy
US, Brand Value Development. Earlier, in
2001, he began working in the music industry,
responsible for public relations and marketing
of P60. He became involved, and sometimes
still is involved in tour bookings and festival
programming. In 2004, he made a definitive
switch to another creative industry: design.

Starting off as public relations manager
for BNO, he now is responsible for all
communications, publications and
media of this association, amongst
which are the websites, the weekly news
digest Nieuwsberichten and design
business magazine Vormberichten.

# icograda
# IDA

**International Council
of Graphic Design Associations**
A Partner of the International
Design Alliance

**Design Week**

www.designweek.co.uk

**BNO/Vormberichten**

www.bno.nl

IDENTITY

**TITLE**
ARCA
**COMPANY**
the design shop
**CLIENT**
ARCA Architects
**ART DIRECTOR**
Dionysis Livanis
**COUNTRY**
Greece

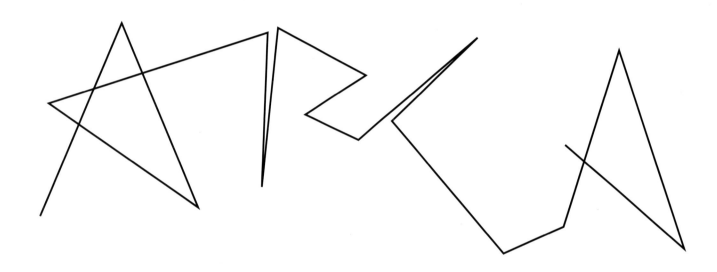

**01.**
TITLE
Alumni ESP
COMPANY
El Paso,
Galería de Comunicación
CLIENT
ESP -Escuela Superior
de Publicidad-
COUNTRY
Spain

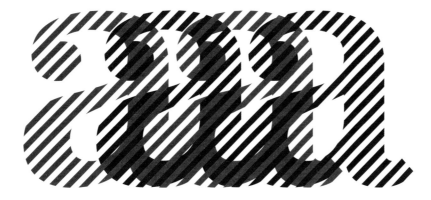

**02.**
TITLE
Zaragoza 2016
COMPANY
Cubo Diseño
CLIENT
Ayuntamiento
de Zaragoza
COUNTRY
Spain

**Zaragoza 2016**
Capital Europea de la Cultura

## 01.
**TITLE**
Portuguese Republic Centennial
**COMPANY**
FBA. – Ferrand,
Bicker & Associados
**CLIENT**
Comissão Nacional Para
As Comemorações Do
Centenário Da República
**COUNTRY**
Portugal

## 02.
**TITLE**
"2" Spaghetti Grafica:
Contemporary Italian Graphic
Design, Second edition
**COMPANY**
ginette caron
**CLIENT**
Ministero della Grafica
**COUNTRY**
Italy

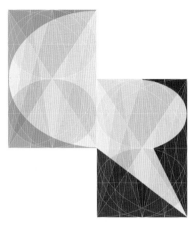

**03.**
TITLE
CastYourArt.com
COMPANY
Grafikdesign Stefanie
Schöffmann
CLIENT
KA21 GmbH
COUNTRY
Austria

**04.**
TITLE
Visual Appearance of the 250th
anniversary / Bavarian Academy
of Sciences and Humanities
COMPANY
xhoch4 | design plus kultur
CLIENT
Bayerische Akademie
der Wissenschaften
COUNTRY
Germany

250 Jahre
Bayerische Akademie
der Wissenschaften

**01.**
**TITLE**
Taxi Vespa scooter
workshop-Barcelona
**COMPANY**
Alexis Rom estudio:::
Taller Vostok
**CLIENT**
Taxi Vespa
**DESIGNERS**
Alexis Rom,
Claude Marzotto
**ILLUSTRATORS**
Alexis Rom,
Claude Marzotto
**COUNTRY**
Spain

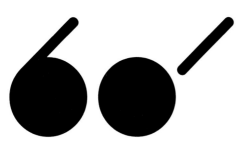

THEATRE OF THE BLIND
AND VISUALLY IMPAIRED
**NEW LIFE**

THEATRICAL COMPANY OF
THE BLIND AND VISUALLY IMPAIRED
**NEW LIFE**

60TH ANNIVERSARY

KAZALIŠTE
SLIJEPIH I SLABOVIDNIH
**NOVI ŽIVOT**

## 02.
**TITLE**
Theatre of the blind
/ 60th anniversary
**COMPANY**
Laboratorium
**CLIENT**
Theatre of the blind
and visually impaired 'New life'
**DESIGNERS**
Orsat Frankovic
Zelimir Boras
**ART DIRECTOR**
Orsat Frankovic
**CREATIVE DIRECTORS**
Orsat Frankovic
Ivana Vucic
**COUNTRY**
Croatia

## 03.
**TITLE**
Kontext Architektur
**COMPANY**
BergmannStudios
**CLIENT**
Kontext Architektur Hüsen
Und Düll Partnerschaft
**COUNTRY**
Germany

# Kontext Architektur

# Kontext Architektur

**01.**
**TITLE**
Gas-Union redesign
**COMPANY**
Josephine Prokop - corporate branding
**CLIENT**
Gas-Union
**COUNTRY**
Germany

**02.**
**TITLE**
CityPost Identity
**COMPANY**
20-20 Vision Ltd
**CLIENT**
CityPost
**COUNTRY**
Ireland

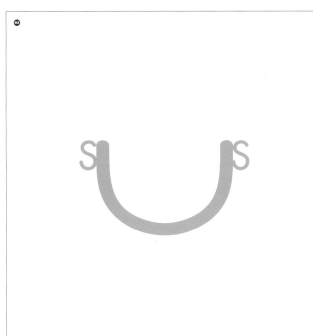

BIJEEN

SINDS 2010

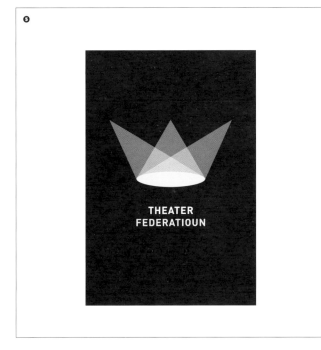

**FINALIST**
COMPANY LOGO

**01.**
TITLE
Venom Identity
COMPANY
form
CLIENT
Venom films
COUNTRY
Ireland

**02.**
TITLE
Su's Ceramics
COMPANY
Haas Design
CLIENT
Susan Kemp Ceramics
COUNTRY
United Kingdom

**03.**
TITLE
Bijeen
COMPANY
vijf890
CLIENT
Bijeen
COUNTRY
The Netherlands

**04.**
TITLE
BCT
COMPANY
Linie 3 - Design - &
Werbeagentur GmbH
CLIENT
BCT - Best Communication
Technology
COUNTRY
Austria

**05.**
TITLE
Theater Federation
COMPANY
Vidale-Gloesener
CLIENT
Theater Federatioun
URL
www.theater.lu
COUNTRY
Luxembourg

# GOLD
## BRAND IMPLEMENTATION

**TITLE**
Brecht Festival Augsburg 2010
**COMPANY**
KW Neun Grafikagentur
**CLIENT**
Kulturamt der Stadt Augsburg
**DESIGNER**
Markus Hasel
Christoph Sauter
Daniel Schäfer
**ART DIRECTOR**
Mara Weyel
**CREATIVE DIRECTOR**
Artur Gulbicki
**COUNTRY**
www.brechtfestival.de
**COUNTRY**
Germany

It's an informal identity which can be easily adapted to different uses through a modular system. It's consistent and recognisable, and it uses a strong and contemporary visual language to promote Bertol Brecht to a wider audience, and in particular to a younger audience.

# GOLD
BRAND IMPLEMENTATION

**TITLE**
Letterlab
**COMPANY**
Strange Attractors Design
**CLIENTS**
Graphic Design Museum, Breda, The Netherlands
**DESIGNERS**
Ryan Pescatore Frisk, Catelijne Van Middelkoop
**ART DIRECTORS**
Ryan Pescatore Frisk, Catelijne Van Middelkoop
**CREATIVE DIRECTORS**
Ryan Pescatore Frisk, Catelijne Van Middelkoop
**COPY WRITER**
Marieke Van Oudheusden
**EDITORS**
Ryan Pescatore Frisk, Catelijne Van Middelkoop
**ILLUSTRATORS**
Ryan Pescatore Frisk, Catelijne Van Middelkoop
**TYPE DESIGN**
Ryan Pescatore Frisk, Catelijne Van Middelkoop
**GAME DESIGN**
Ryan Pescatore Frisk, Catelijne Van Middelkoop
**SPATIAL DESIGN**
Ryan Pescatore Frisk, Catelijne Van Middelkoop
**URL**
www.letterlab.com
**COUNTRY**
The Netherlands

This exhibition's design does a fantastic job in getting parents and children interested in letters, and it does it in an engaging and fresh way, without being patronizing. Letterlab is visually stimulating and rich, and goes beyond the clichés, showing that children can enjoy complexity when it makes sense.

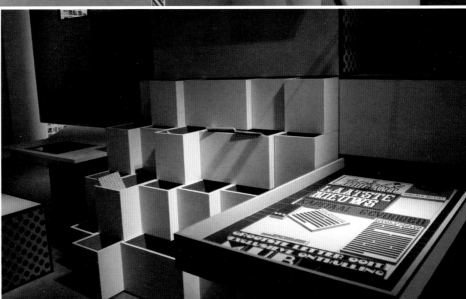

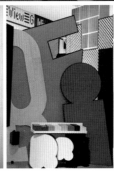

## BRONZE
BRAND IMPLEMENTATION

**TITLE**
<Fishead(
**COMPANY**
Jan Šabach Design
**CLIENT**
<Fishead(
**URL**
www.fishead-movie.com
**COUNTRY**
Czech Republic

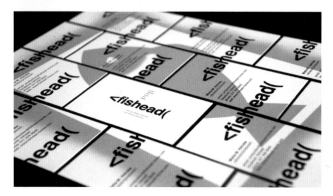

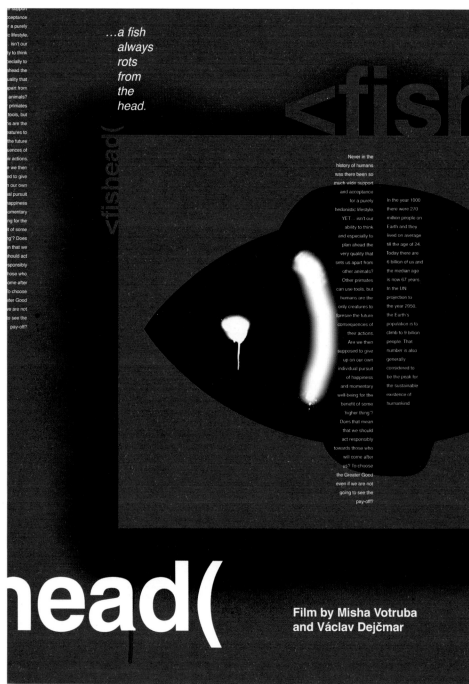

**TITLE**
Die freien Anaesthesisten
**COMPANY**
Hesse Design
**CLIENTS**
Die freien Anaesthesisten
**COUNTRY**
Germany

**die**freien**a**naesthesisten

business cards

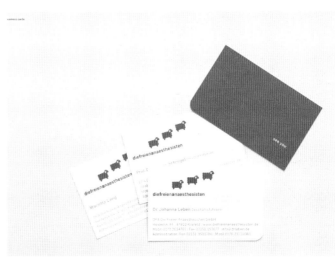

note papers

# BRONZE
## BRAND IMPLEMENTATION

**TITLE**
PURE
**COMPANY**
Neue Design Studio
**CLIENT**
The PURE Water Company
**URL**
purewater.gapt.no
**COUNTRY**
Norway

# P
# U
# R
# E.®

WATER

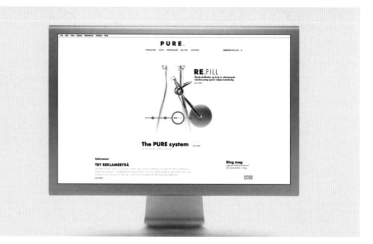

**TITLE**
The 4th Biennial of Slovene
Visual Communications
**COMPANY**
IlovarStritar d.o.o.
**CLIENTS**
Brumen Foundation
**COUNTRY**
Slovenia

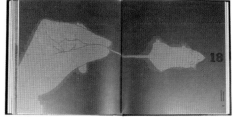

**TITLE**
Katowice 2016
**COMPANY**
Gobranding.eu
**CLIENT**
The City of Katowice
**COUNTRY**
Poland

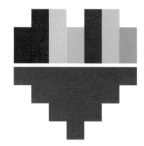

# KATOWICE

Candidate for European
Capital of Culture

## 2016

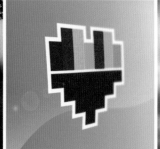

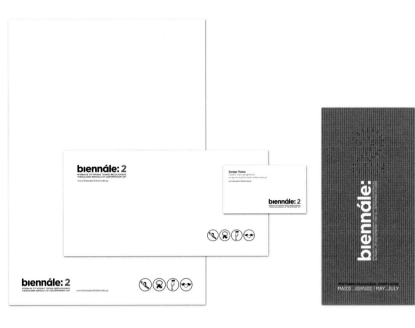

**FINALIST**
BRAND IMPLEMENTATION

**TITLE**
Biennale 2
**COMPANY**
Red Creative
**CLIENT**
Greek State Museum
of Contemporary Art
**URL**
www.thessalonikibiennale.gr
**COUNTRY**
Greece

**TITLE**
Willie's World Class Cacao
**COMPANY**
Taxi Studio
**CLIENT**
El Tesoro
**URL**
www.williescacao.com
**COUNTRY**
United Kingdom

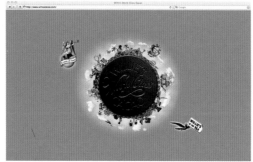

**TITLE**
Oerol identity
and campagne 2009
**COMPANY**
Dietwee
**CLIENT**
Oerol
**URL**
oerol.nl
**COUNTRY**
The Netherlands

**TITLE**
National Technical
Library manual
**COMPANY**
Laboratoř, Petr Babák
**CLIENT**
Národní Technická knihovna
(National Technical Library)
**URL**
www.techlib.cz
**COUNTRY**
Czech Republic

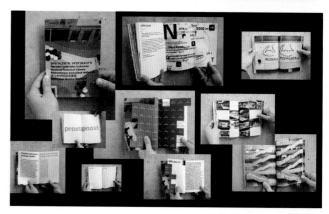
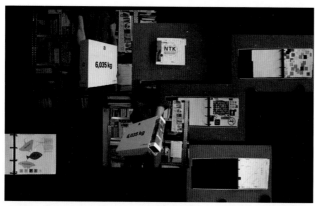

**TITLE**
La Biennale di Venezia -
Fari Mondi (Making Worlds)
**COMPANY**
Stockholm Design Lab
**CLIENT**
La Biennale di Venezia
**COUNTRY**
Sweden

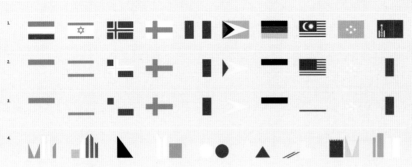

# FINALIST
## BRAND IMPLEMENTATION

**TITLE**
Scheer
**COMPANY**
Circus. Büro für Kommunikation
und Gestaltung
**CLIENT**
Scheer Schuhe , Wien
**URL**
www.scheer.at
**COUNTRY**
Austria

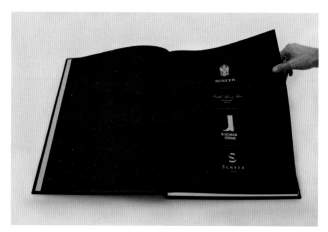

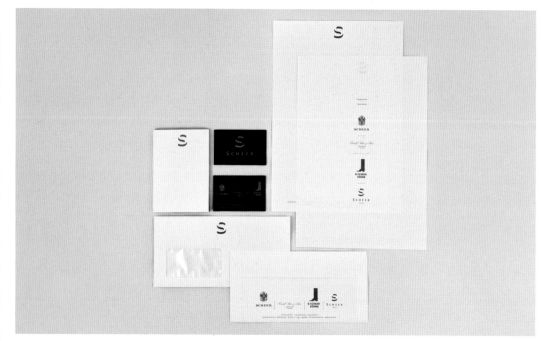

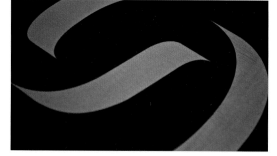

**ERASMUS**
IN ROTTERDAM

**FINALIST**
BRAND IMPLEMENTATION

**TITLE**
Erasmus in Rotterdam
**COMPANY**
ping-pong Design
**CLIENT**
Rotterdam Festivals
**COUNTRY**
Netherlands

# GOLD
COMPANY IMPLEMENTATION

**TITLE**
De Balie
**COMPANY**
Lava
**CLIENT**
De Balie
**DESIGNER**
Ruben Pater
**COUNTRY**
The Netherlands

De Balie's identity system reflects the richness and diversity of the activities of this cultural centre. It combines the individuality of each event while maintaining an overall coherence in the communication of what De Balie is. It's clever and easily applied to different uses: it can become very strong, as in posters, or leave room for other information, as in the centre's programmes. It works perfectly without the need to add images, which at times would have been too obvious a solution.

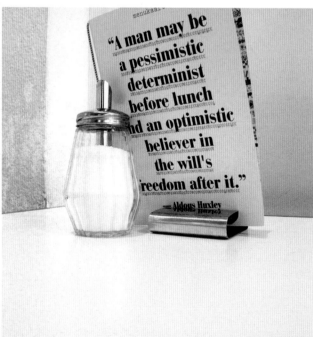

oktober
2009

ma 12 okt

# HET STRIJD-
# TONEEL:
## *HET LEGER,*
## *DE NATIE EN*
## *DE LEIDERS*

za 17 okt

# HET GROTE
# ONVRUCHT-
# BAARHEID
# SOUPER

CLUB INTERBELLUM

do 22 okt

# HOW TO
# KILL
# MUGABE

vanaf wo 14 okt

FW: FOTOGRAFIE

# City
# Visions
# Europe

do 1 okt

# Cineville
# Talkshow:
# Moon

elke dag

**Uit eigen keuken:**
## Paté van
## kwartel,
## fazant
## en kip
## met toast

# debalie

programma
oktober 2009

**TITLE**
Brno Philharmonic – Corporate
Design
**COMPANY**
Side2
**CLIENT**
Brno Philharmonic
**DESIGNER**
Marius Corradini
**ART DIRECTOR**
Tomáš Machek
**CREATIVE DIRECTOR**
Tomáš Machek
**PHOTOGRAPHER**
Marek Novotný
**URL**
www.filharmonie-brno.cz
**COUNTRY**
Czech Republic

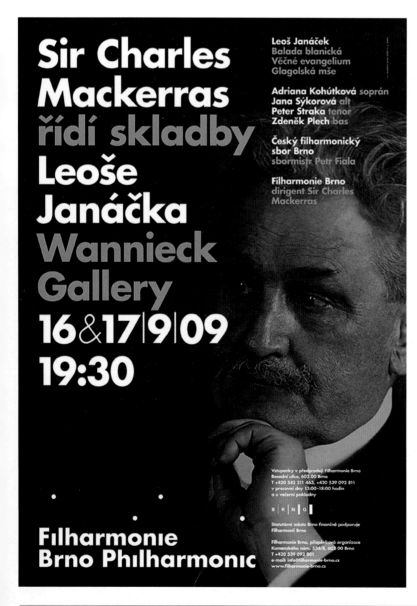

Bedřich
Wolfgang
Antonín
Ludwig
Franz

Bedřich
Wolfgang
Antonín
Ludwig
Franz

Filharmonie
Brno Philharmonic

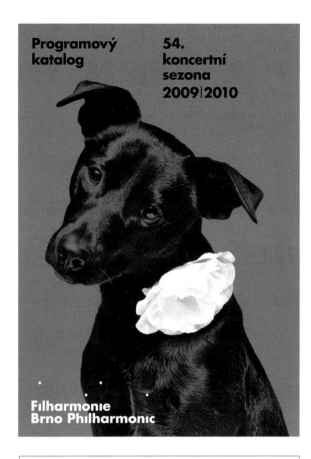

Programový
katalog

54.
koncertní
sezona
2009|2010

Filharmonie
Brno Philharmonic

Zdenek Merta
Ze starého světa
Leonard Bernstein
Věk úzkosti
Wannieck Gallery
21|1|2010
19:30

Ladislav Doležel klavír
Filharmonie Brno
dirigent Caspar Richter

Vstupenky v předprodeji
Filharmonie Brno
Besední ulice, 602 00 Brno
T +420 539 092 811
v pracovní dny 13:00–18:00 hodin
a u večerní pokladny

Filharmonie Brno
příspěvková organizace
Komenského nám. 534/8, 602 00 Brno
T +420 539 092 801
info@filharmonie-brno.cz
www.filharmonie-brno.cz

Filharmonie
Brno Philharmonic

Statutární město Brno finančně podporuje
Filharmonii Brno

Filharmonie
Brno Philharmonic

Filharmonie
Brno Philharmonic

David Mareček

PF 2010    Šťastný nový rok | Happy New Year | Glückliches neues Jahr | Bonne année

Filharmonie
Brno Philharmonic

## SILVER
COMPANY IMPLEMENTATION

**TITLE**
CHEF.
**COMPANY**
rincón2 medien gmbh
**CLIENT**
Churfrsten Group
**DESIGNERS**
Martina Hartmann, Robert Hard
**ART DIRECTOR**
Martina Hartmann
**CREATIVE DIRECTORS**
Robert Hardt,
Matthias Rincón
**COPYWRITER**
Robert Hardt
**EDITOR**
Robert Hardt
**COUNTRY**
Germany

# SILVER
COMPANY IMPLEMENTATION

**TITLE**
RUBENS Guesthouse
**COMPANY**
wortwerk
**CLIENT**
RUBENS Guesthouse
**ART DIRECTOR**
Verena Panholzer
**CREATIVE DIRECTOR**
Christian Satek
**ILLUSTRATOR**
Heri Irawan
**URL**
www.rubens-gasthaus.at
**COUNTRY**
Austria

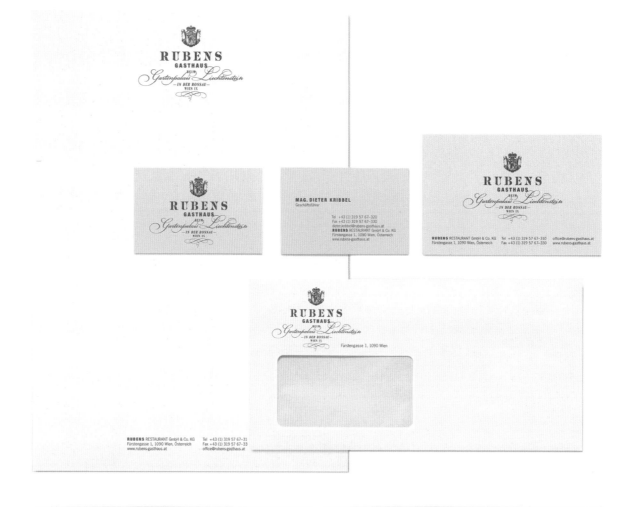

# BRONZE
COMPANY IMPLEMENTATION

**TITLE**
Nomint
**COMPANY**
Beetroot Design Group
**CLIENT**
Nomint
**COUNTRY**
Greece

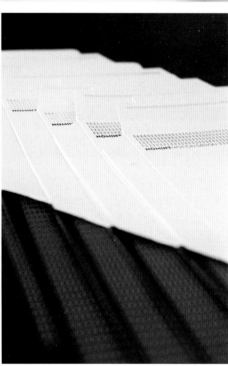

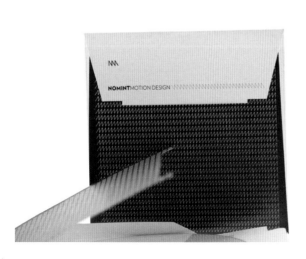

# STADSSCHOUWBURG UTRECHT

**BRONZE**
COMPANY IMPLEMENTATION

**TITLE**
Utrecht City Theatre
**COMPANY**
Edenspiekermann Amsterdam
**CLIENT**
Stadsschouwburg Utrecht
**URL**
www.stadsschouwburg-utrecht.nl
**COUNTRY**
The Netherlands

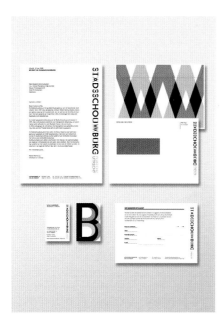

**TITLE**
NHL
**COMPANY**
Koeweiden Postma
**CLIENT**
NHL Hogeschool
**COUNTRY**
The Netherlands

**TITLE**
Mozarteumorchester Salzburg
**COMPANY**
Parole GmbH
**CLIENT**
Mozarteumorchester Salzburg
**COUNTRY**
Germany

**TITLE**
Noord Nederlandse Dans
**COMPANY**
Dietwee
**CLIENT**
Noord Nederlandse Dans
**URL**
noordnederlandsedans.com
**COUNTRY**
Netherlands

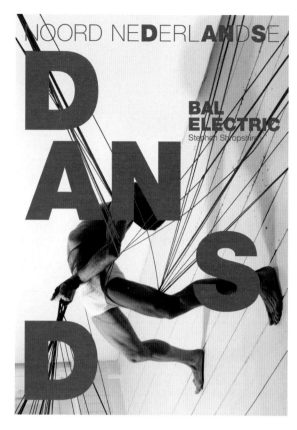

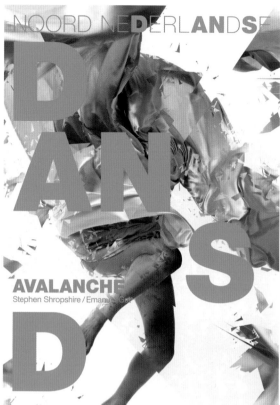

**FINALIST**
COMPANY IMPLEMENTATION

**TITLE**
Vredenburg Identity
**COMPANY**
Dietwee
**CLIENT**
Vredenbrug
**URL**
vredenburg.nl
**COUNTRY**
The Netherlands

# FINALIST
## COMPANY IMPLEMENTATION

**TITLE**
TOLIX identity
**COMPANY**
Superscript
**CLIENT**
TOLIX
**COUNTRY**
France

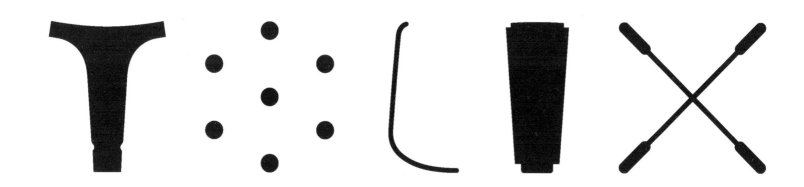

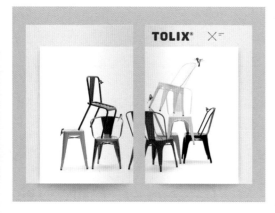

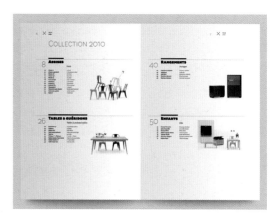

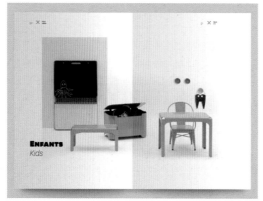
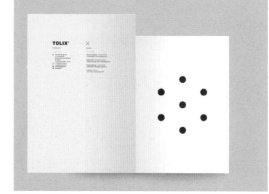

**TITLE**
National Theater
**COMPANY**
bleed
**CLIENT**
National Theatre Oslo
**COUNTRY**
Norway

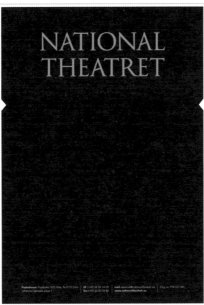

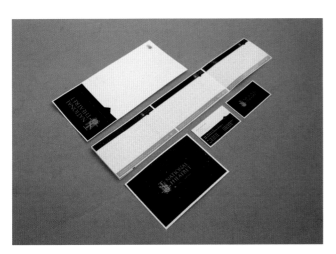

PUBLICATIONS

**TITLE**
Haags Wonen 2008
**COMPANY**
Fabrique Communicatie
en Design
**CLIENT**
Haag Wonen
**DESIGNER**
Martijn Maas
**ART DIRECTOR**
Simone van Rijn
**COPYWRITERS**
Rozatekst, Corianna Roza
**ILLUSTRATOR**
Martijn Maas
**PHOTOGRAPHER**
Boudewijn Bollman
**PROJECT MANAGER**
Maartje Wensing
**COUNTRY**
The Netherlands

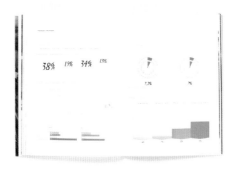

Annual report designers have always tried to add value to data and information by adding an extra layer, which often turns out to be beautiful but disconnected from the main content. The Haags Wonen Annual Report 2008 manages to intertwine the two levels, making intelligent use of text, imagery (photographs from the neighbourhoods involved), information (presented both in "data-driven" and "emotional" formats) and graphics (pattern derived from the shapes of the different districts on the map). An outstanding typography and strong attention to the overall rhythm make this book a beautiful object; the jury also appreciated seeing such a high level of design concern for a housing association.

**TITLE**
Nedap 2008
**COMPANY**
Studio Kluif
**COUNTRY**
Netherlands

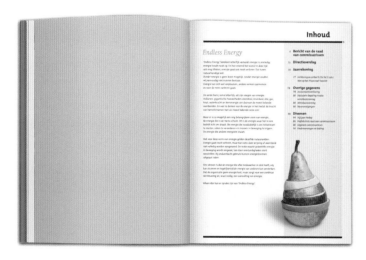

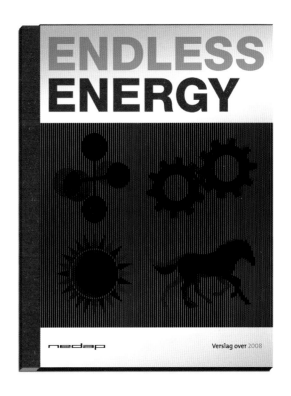

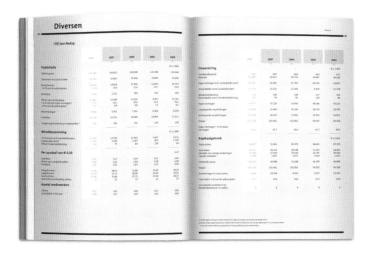

## SILVER
ANNUAL REPORT

**TITLE**
Zambon Value Report 2008
**COMPANY**
Rumore Bianco SRL
**CLIENT**
Zambon
**DESIGNER**
Alexandra Gredler
**CREATIVE DIRECTORS**
Micaela Perego
Linda Ronzoni
Alfred Drago
**PHOTOGRAPHER**
Cesare Cicardini
**COUNTRY**
Italy

**TITLE**
META, Consultancy
and information centre
for young migrants
**COMPANY**
Štěpánka Bláhovcová
**CLIENT**
META, Consultancy
and information centre
for young migrants
**DESIGNER**
Štěpánka Bláhovcová
**EDITOR**
Zuzana Vodnanska
**ILLUSTRATOR**
Štěpánka Bláhovcová
**PHOTOS**
archive of META,
Consultancy and information
centre for young migrants
**COUNTRY**
Czech Republic

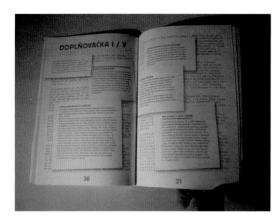

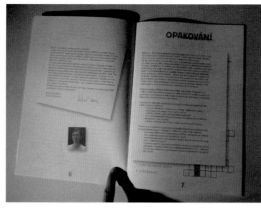

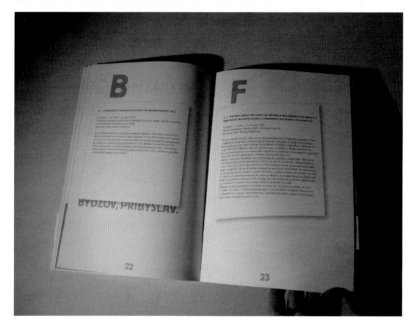

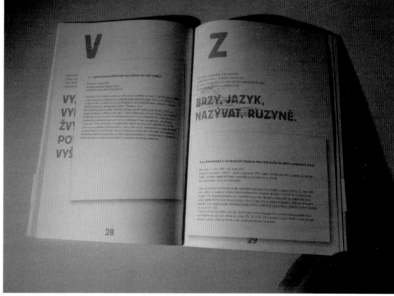

**TITLE**
Schönheit
**COMPANY**
Maksimovic & partners
**CLIENT**
SIPA Unternehmer Beratung
**COUNTRY**
Germany

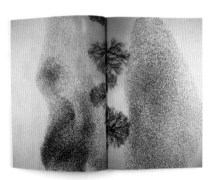

# BRONZE
ANNUAL REPORT

**TITLE**
Lagebericht 2008
**COMPANY**
Wollzelle GmbH
**CLIENT**
Wiener Hauskrankenpflege
(WHS)
**COUNTRY**
Austria

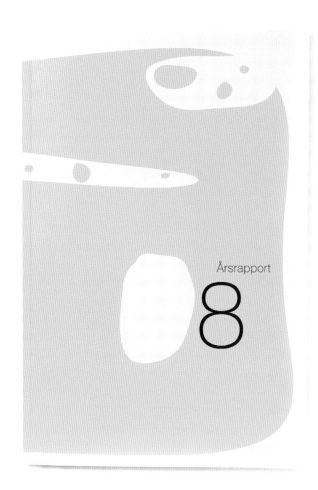

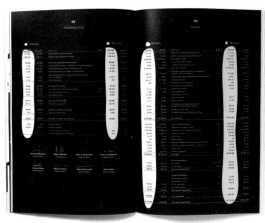

**TITLE**
Sandnes Sparebank 08
**COMPANY**
fasett
**CLIENTS**
Sandnes Sparebank
**COUNTRY**
Norway

**TITLE**
Vlehan 2008 'Cradle to Cradle'
**COMPANY**
52 graden noorderbreedte
**CLIENTS**
Vlehan
**COUNTRY**
The Netherlands

# SILVER
BOOK COVER

**TITLE**
Minotauro
**COMPANY**
FBA. – Ferrand,
Bicker & Associados
**CLIENT**
EDIÜES 70
**DESIGNERS**
Ana Boavida
Joï Bicker
**CREATIVE DIRECTOR**
Joï Bicker
**ILLUSTRATOR**
Ana Boavida
**COUNTRY**
Portugal

**TITLE**
Where there is smoke,
there is fire
**COMPANY**
Trapped in suburbia
**CLIENT**
City of the Hague
**DESIGNER**
Debora Schiltmans
**ART DIRECTORS**
Cuby Gerards
Karin Langeveld
**CREATIVE DIRECTORS**
Cuby Gerards
Karin Langeveld
Debora Schiltmans
**COPYWRITER**
Jaap Huisman
**EDITOR**
Jaap Huisman
**COUNTRY**
The Netherlands

**TITLE**
A5
**COMPANY**
mueller,weiland GbR
**CLIENT**
Lars Mueller Publishers,
FH Duesseldorf
**CREATIVE DIRECTOR**
Jens Mueller
**EDITOR**
Jens Mueller
**COUNTRY**
Germany

**TITLE**
Series of book Karakter
**DESIGNER**
Przemek Dębowski
**CLIENT**
Wydawnictwo Karakter
**COUNTRY**
Poland

TITLE
Eduardo Mendoza 's books
COMPANY
Parastudio
CLIENT
"Znak" Publishing House
COUNTRY
Poland

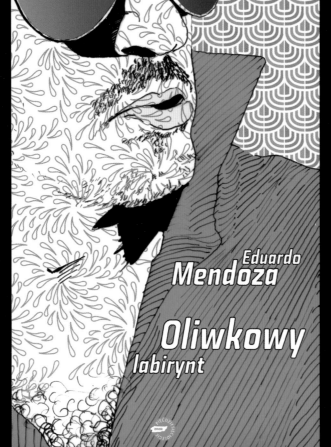

**TITLE**
Biennale 2
**COMPANY**
Red Creative
**CLIENT**
State Museum
Of Contemporary Art
**URL**
www.thessalonikibiennale.gr
**COUNTRY**
Greece

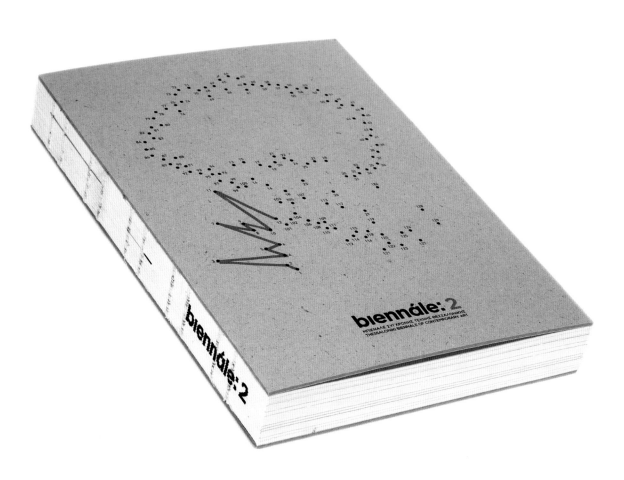

# GOLD
BOOK LAYOUT

**TITLE**
TEDxAmsterdam-Breakthrough
**COMPANY**
SILO
**CLIENT**
TEDxAmsterdam
**PHOTOGRAPHERS**
Ivo van der Bent
Nadine Stijns
**COUNTRY**
The Netherlands

It's a challenge to live up to the reputation of TED events, which are well-known in the online world, with a book, but TEDx Amsterdam does just that. The illustrations give a strong overall consistency, while the interspersed booklets add a surprise element that enriches the main story. The layout is very clear with elements hinting at something that goes beyond the page and the talks section is intuitively highlighted by the change of paper.

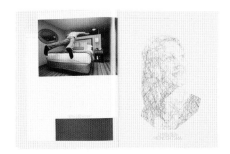
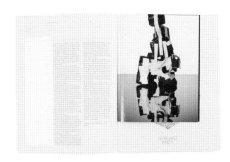

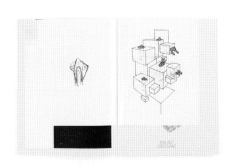

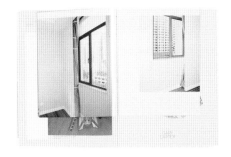
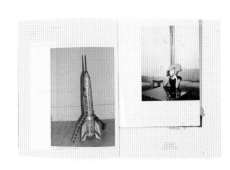
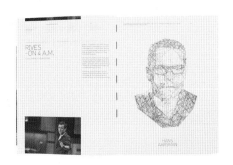

# GOLD
BOOK LAYOUT

**TITLE**
Many hands make churches withstand / Práce jako na kostele
**COMPANY**
Štěpánka Bláhovcová
**CLIENT**
Lag Czech West Local Partnership
**DESIGNER**
Štěpánka Bláhovcová
**COPYWRITERS**
Štěpánka Bláhovcová, Lag Czech West Local Partnership, Faculty of art and design - University of Jan Evangelista Purkyně in Ústi nad Labem
**EDITORS**
Kateřina Kvasničková
Zbyněk Sedláček
**ILLUSTRATOR**
Štěpánka Bláhovcová
**PHOTOGRAPHER**
Štěpánka Bláhovcová
**COUNTRY**
Czech Republic

The design achieves an excellent integration of text and images; the reader can read the book through these two layers that support each other. The concept is well thought-out, and the result is a visually attractive book, rich in content but never overdone.

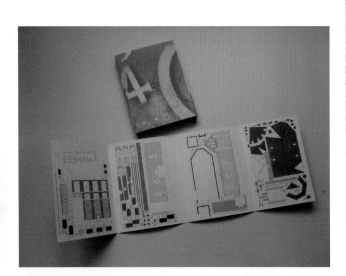

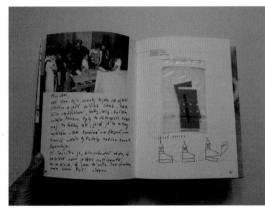

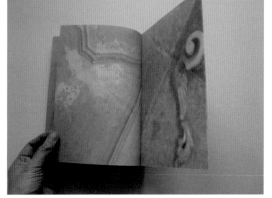

**TITLE**
BILLY - 30 Jahre jung/30 Jahre alt
**COMPANY**
Heine/Lenz/Zizka Projekte GmbH
**CLIENT**
IKEA Germany
**ART DIRECTORS**
Joel Carneiro
Katrin Schacke
**CREATIVE DIRECTOR**
Heine/Lenz/Zizka
**COPYWRITER**
Nina Puri
**EDITORS**
IKEA Germany
Verlag Zweitausendeins
**ILLUSTRATOR**
Dorine de Vos
**PHOTOGRAPHERS**
Martin Grothmaak
Tom Ziora
**COUNTRY**
Germany

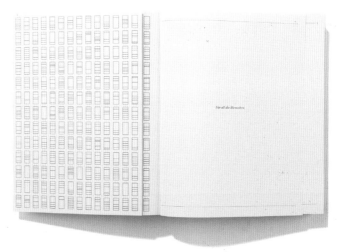

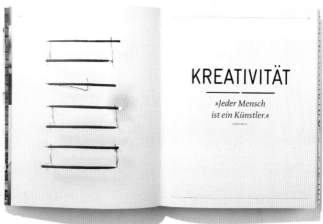

**TITLE**
Albert Nufer, Typotron-Heft 27
**COMPANY**
TGG Hafen Senn Stieger
**CLIENT**
Typotron
**COUNTRY**
Switzerland

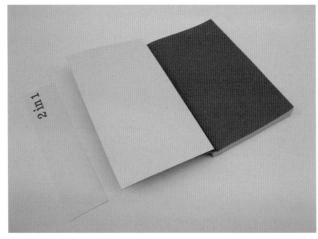

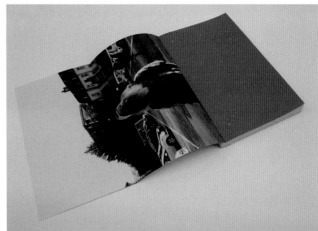

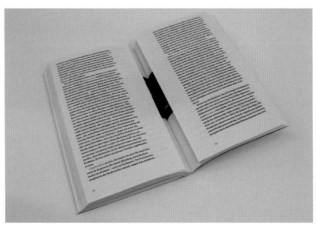

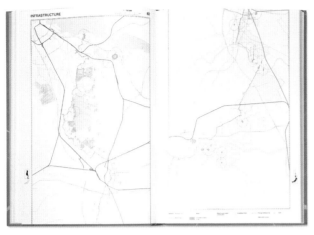

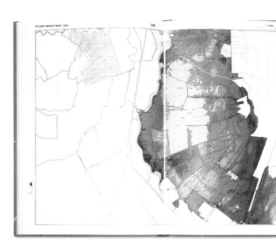

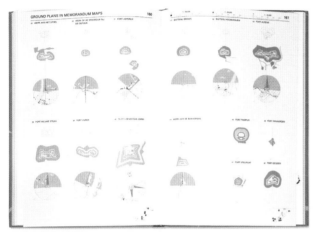

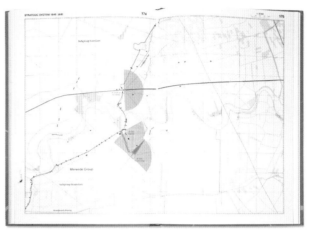

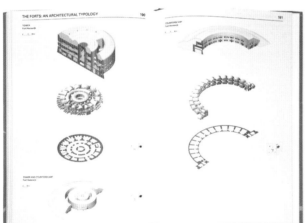

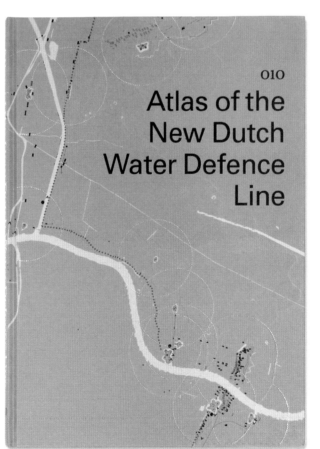

**TITLE**
Atlas of the New Dutch Water
Defence Line
**COMPANY**
010 Publishers
**CLIENT**
The Netherlands Architecture
Fund and the Nieuwe Hollandse
Waterlinie Project Office
**COUNTRY**
The Netherlands

# BRONZE
BOOK LAYOUT

**TITLE**
Dear Ms Brauch, … - Schicksal
und Schönheit der gebrochenen
Schriftformen
**COMPANY**
FH JOANNEUM Graz
**CLIENT**
FH JOANNEUM Graz
**COUNTRY**
Austria

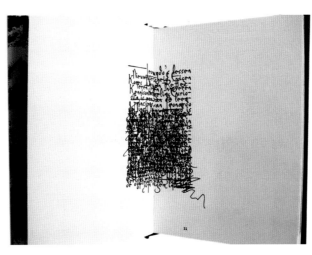

**TITLE**
Leonardo'S Lessen
**COMPANY**
Van Riet Ontwerpers
**CLIENT**
Cinop
**COUNTRY**
The Netherlands

**TITLE**
Lechners Nautische Bibliothek
**COMPANY**
Kochan & Partner
**CLIENT**
ProkonVerlag München
**COUNTRY**
Germany

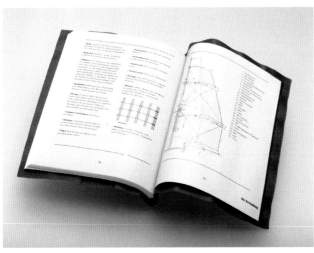

# FINALIST
## BOOK LAYOUT

**TITLE**
Hi Brandbook
**COMPANY**
Trapped in suburbia
**CLIENT**
Hi
**COUNTRY**
The Netherlands

**TITLE**
Nyugat Picture-Book
**COMPANY**
Cadmium Bt.
**CLIENT**
Petofi Literary Museum,
Budapest, Hungary
**COUNTRY**
Hungary

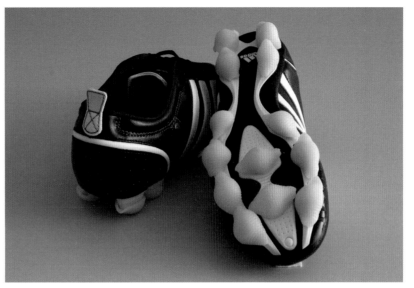

**TITLE**
Food Design Xl
**COMPANY**
honey and bunny productions
**COUNTRY**
Austria

**TITLE**
Flying Clipper Loggbok
**COMPANY**
Wettre förlag
**CLIENT**
Jonas Wettre
Staffan Wettre
Gunnar Stenström
**COUNTRY**
Sweden

**TITLE**
Invisible men
**COMPANY**
eindeloos
**CLIENT**
Patricia Kaersenhout
**COUNTRY**
The Netherlands

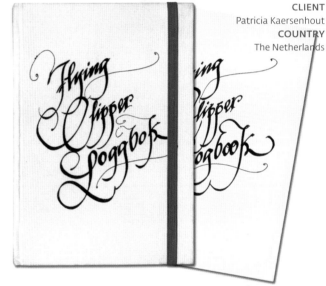

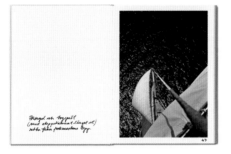

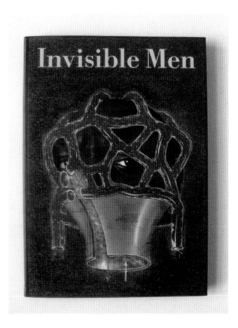

**TITLE**
To Cover Edition
**COMPANY**
JUNO
**CLIENT**
Peyer Graphic GmbH
**DESIGNERS**
Wolfgang Greter
Nicole Klein
Sebastian Schneider
Barbara Schwitzke
**ART DIRECTORS**
Nicole Klein
Sebastian Schneider
**CREATIVE DIRECTORS**
Wolfgang Greter
Björn Lux
**EDITOR**
Juno
**COUNTRY**
Germany

**TITLE**
Soul:made guide
**COMPANY**
Barlock
**CLIENT**
Soul:made: a communication
consultancy agency
**DESIGNER**
Jesse Skolnik
**CREATIVE DIRECTORS**
Marc van Bokhoven
Jesse Skolnik
**COUNTRY**
The Netherlands

... 'and what is the use of a
book,' thought Alice, 'without
pictures or conversation?'

QUESTION
EVERYTHING

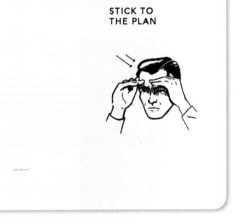

STICK TO
THE PLAN

**TITLE**
Dua Brochure »Einblicke«
**COMPANY**
Raffael Stüken /
Büro für Grafik Design
**COUNTRY**
Germany

**TITLE**
Traces of Men
**COMPANY**
Büro Alba
**CLIENT**
Discovery Communications
Europe
**COUNTRY**
Germany

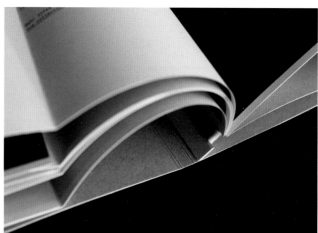

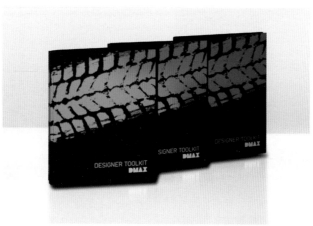
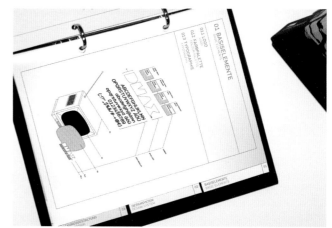

**TITLE**
Klang = Skulptur
**COMPANY**
Neeser & Müller
**CLIENT**
Verein Neue Musik Rümlingen
**COUNTRY**
Switzerland

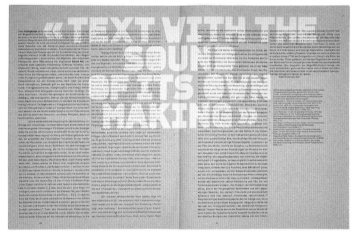

**TITLE**
Leica M
**COMPANY**
argonauten G2 GmbH -
a member of Grey | G2 Group
**CLIENT**
Leica Camera AG
**DESIGNER**
Sabine Brinkmann
**ART DIRECTOR**
Sabine Brinkmann
**CREATIVE DIRECTORS**
Anita Stoll
Felix Drichen
**COPYWRITERS**
Anita Stoll
Sabine Weber
**PHOTOGRAPHER**
Maik Scharfscheer
**ACCOUNT DIRECTORS**
Maik Hofmann
Silvana Meyer
**STRATEGIC PLANNING**
Judd Labarthe
**COUNTRY**
Germany

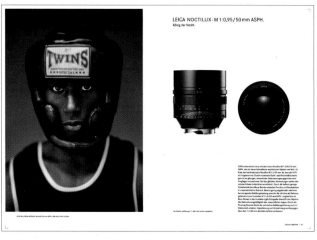

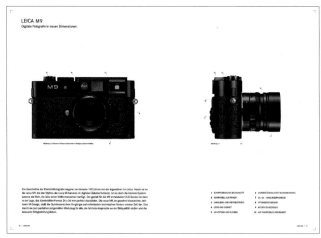

Heine Warnecke Design GmbH

CLIENTS
A. Viani Importe Gmbh

DESIGNERS
Dirk Heine
Cord Warnecke

ART DIRECTOR
Dirk Heine

CREATIVE DIRECTOR
Dirk Heine

COPYWRITER
A. Viani Importe Gmbh

EDITOR
A. Viani Importe Gmbh

PHOTOGRAPHERS
Dirk Heine
Thomas Klawunn

COUNTRY
Germany

**TITLE**
Waste/Muell - Urban Plus
**COMPANY**
MAAS + CO
**CLIENT**
OTTOEntsorgungssysteme
GmbH - Urban Plus
**COUNTRY**
Germany

Pinto

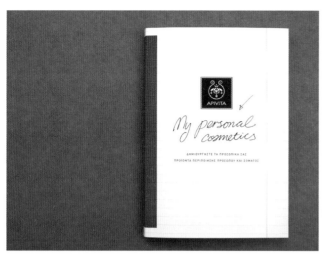
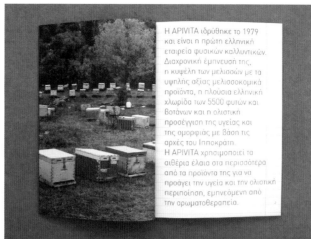

**TITLE**
Apivita Personal catalogue
**COMPANY**
Dimopoulos Karatzas
**CLIENT**
Apivita
**COUNTRY**
Greece

# BRONZE
PRODUCT CATALOGUE

**TITLE**
Nodus - High Design Rugs 2009
**COMPANY**
normat
**CLIENT**
Il Piccolo
**COUNTRY**
Italy

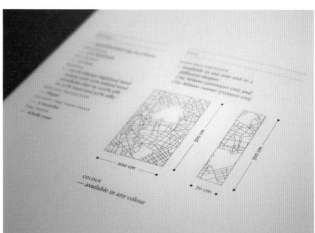

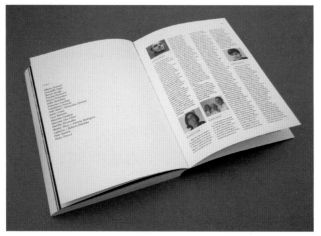

**TITLE**
Terre d'Hermès - Press Kit
**COMPANY**
undo-redo
**CLIENT**
Hermès
**COUNTRY**
France

**TITLE**
The Fascination of Hunting
**COMPANY**
Argonauten G2 GmbH -
a member of Grey | G2 Group
**CLIENT**
Leica Camera AG
**COUNTRY**
Germany

**TITLE**
Imprenta Real.
Fonts of Spanish Typography
**COMPANY**
Sanchez/Lacasta
**CLIENTS**
Spanish Ministry
of Foreign Affairs. AECID
**COUNTRY**
Spain

The typographic design goes perfectly with the subject, without being overwhelming, creating a dialogue between text which is meant to be read and text which is meant to be looked at (the historical type specimens). Every design choice is appropriate, from paper to binding and typography. The dividing pages for every chapter give this book a perfect rhythm.

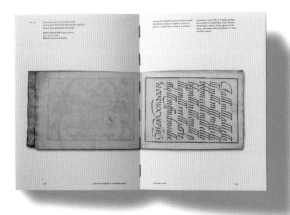

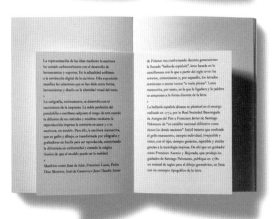

**TITLE**
Ska
**COMPANY**
3group
**CLIENT**
Galeria Wozownia
**ART DIRECTOR**
Ryszard Bienert
**PHOTOGRAPHER**
Studio Nelec
**COUNTRY**
Poland

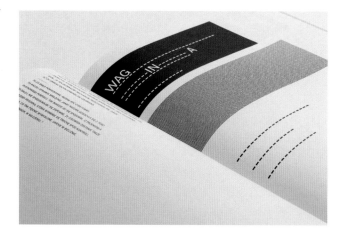

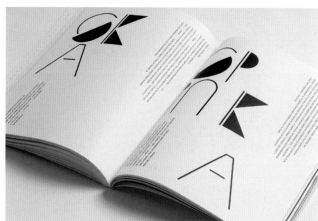

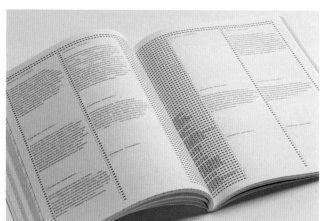

**TITLE**
Ton of Holland
Contemporary Embriodery
**COMPANY**
Dennis Koot & Ton Hoogerwerf
**CLIENT**
Thieme Art
**DESIGNERS**
Dennis Koot
Ton Hoogerwerf
**COPYWRITERS**
Roos van Put
Mattias Duyves
**EDITOR**
Marloes Waanders
**COUNTRY**
The Netherlands

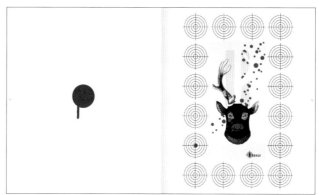

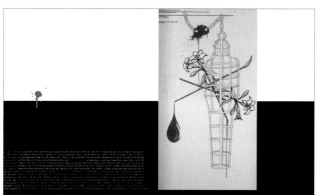

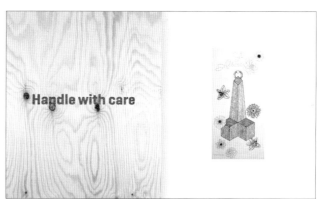

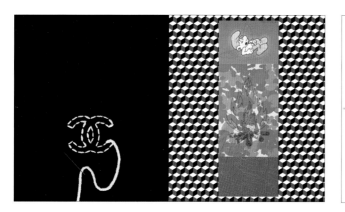

# BRONZE
ARTISTIC CATALOGUE

**TITLE**
Ring frei Kunststudentinnen und
Kunststudenten stellen aus 2009
**COMPANY**
Burghardt&Tank GbR
**CLIENT**
Federal Ministry of Education
and Research, Germany
**COUNTRY**
Germany

**BRONZE**
ARTISTIC CATALOGUE

**TITLE**
Barceló before Barceló 1973-1982
**COMPANY**
Josep Bagà Associats
**CLIENT**
Galaxia Gutenberg Círculo
de Lectores / Fundació Pilar
i Joan Miró a Mallorca /Les
Abattoirs / Arts Santa Mònica
**COUNTRY**
Spain

**TITLE**
Walter Kappacher Schönheit
des Vergehens
**COMPANY**
Linie 3 - Design
& Werbeagentur GmbH
**CLIENT**
Verlag Müry Salzmann
**COUNTRY**
Austria

TITLE
Goalkeeper Forever
COMPANY
3group
CLIENT
Galeria Piekary
COUNTRY
Poland

# FINALIST
ARTISTIC CATALOGUE

**TITLE**
The Truth of Painting
**COMPANY**
3group
**CLIENT**
Galeria Piekary
**COUNTRY**
Poland

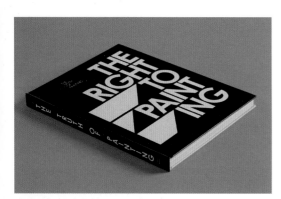

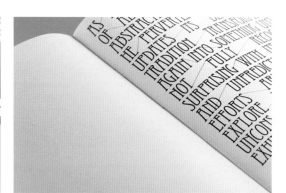

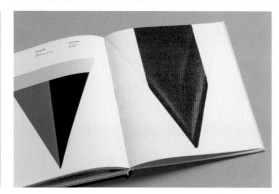

**FINALIST**
ARTISTIC CATALOGUE

**TITLE**
Op Basis van Bas Oudt /
Based on Bas Oudt
**COMPANY**
Claudi Kessels
**CLIENT**
Uitgeverij de Buitenkant
**COUNTRY**
The Netherlands

# SILVER
MAGAZINE

**TITLE**
CITY MAG
**COMPANY**
INgrid
StudioForEditorialDesign
**CLIENT**
Ville De Luxembourg
& Mike Koedinger Editions
**DESIGNER**
Stephanie Poras
**ART DIRECTORS**
Guido Kröger
Vera Capinha Heliodoro
Maxime Pintadu
**CREATIVE DIRECTOR**
Mike Koedinger
**EDITORS**
Duncan Roberts
Deborah Lambolez
Cynthia Winand
**PHOTOGRAPHERS**
Julien Becker,
Andres Lejona
David Laurent
Véronique Kolber
**COUNTRY**
Luxembourg

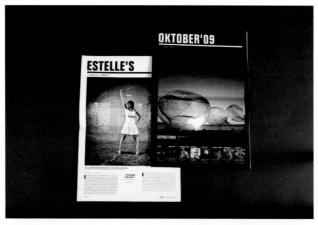

**TITLE**
Brunswick Review
**COMPANY**
JohnstonWorks
**CLIENT**
Brunswick Group LLP
**DESIGNERS**
Kirsten Johnston
Remy Jauffret
Stuart Simpson
Svetlana Andrienko
**CREATIVE DIRECTOR**
Kirsten Johnston
**EDITOR**
Tim Dickson
**PROJECT MANAGER**
Jo Piatek-Stewart
**COUNTRY**
United Kingdom

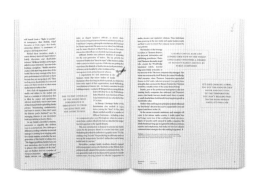

**TITLE**
Notes na 6 tygodni
**COMPANY**
Fundacja Bęc Zmiana
**CLIENT**
Fundacja Bęc Zmiana
**COUNTRY**
Poland

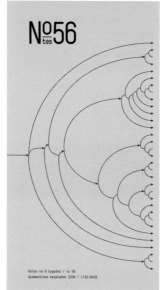

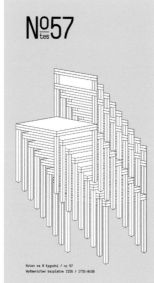

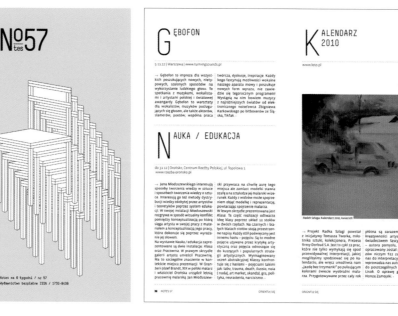

TITLE
Landjäger Magazin
COMPANY
Christian Feurstein
CLIENTS
Landjäger Magazin
COUNTRY
Austria

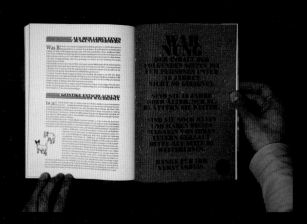

**TITLE**
VIER Magazine
**COMPANY**
Hochschule für Künste Bremen
**COUNTRY**
Germany

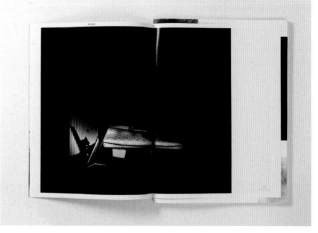

**TITLE**
NICO
**COMPANY**
INgrid
StudioForEditorialDesign
**CLIENT**
Mike Koedinger Editions
**COUNTRY**
Luxembourg

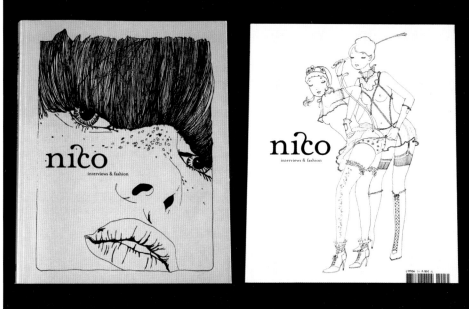

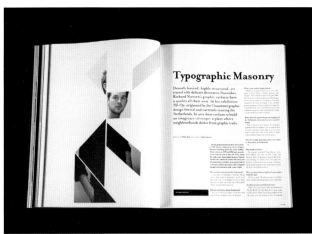

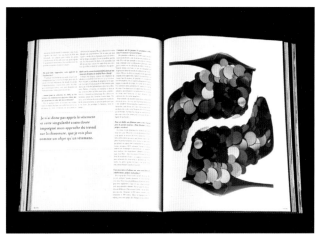

**TITLE**
ŽIVEL
**COMPANY**
ReDesign
**CLIENT**
Dalibor Kubík
**COUNTRY**
Czech Republic

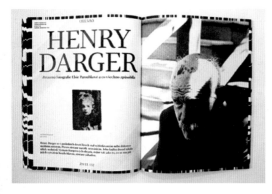

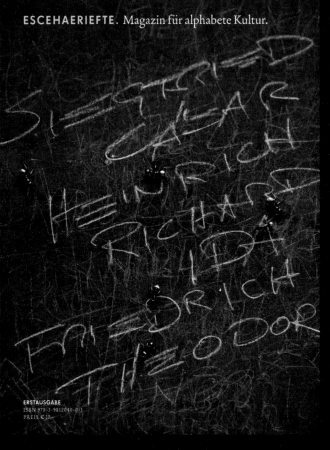

ESCEHAERIEFTE. Magazin für alphabete Kultur.

ERSTAUSGABE
ISBN 978-3-9812040-0-1
PREIS € 10,–

Ist GOtt ein guter Typograf?
Essay zur typografischen Begabung von oben.

TITLE
Escehaeriefte
DESIGNERS
Kochan & Partner
CLIENT
tgm Typographische
Gesellschaft München
COUNTRY
Germany

TITLE
kinki magazine
COMPANY
kinki magazine
CLIENT
Aurum Communication AG
COUNTRY
Switzerland

kinki

kinki

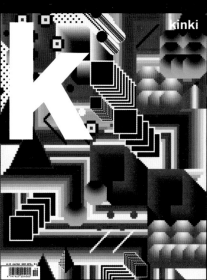

kinki

RESCUED
FROM TIME

**TITLE**
Schampus Magazine
**COMPANY**
BergmannStudios
**CLIENT**
Grüne Jugend Hessen
**COUNTRY**
Germany

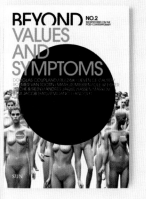

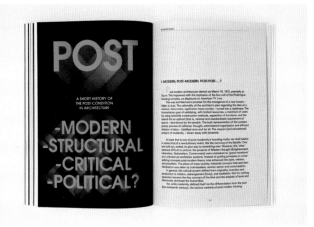

**TITLE**
Beyond
**COMPANY**
Florian Mewes
**COUNTRY**
The Netherlands

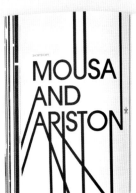

DIGITAL

# GOLD
## PROMOTIONAL SITE

**TITLE**
Call You Back

**COMPANY**
Hinderling Volkart Web Identity

**CLIENT**
Call You Back

**DESIGNER**
Iwan Negro

**ART DIRECTOR**
Iwan Negro
Michael Hinderling

**CREATIVE DIRECTOR**
Michael Hinderling

**COPYWRITER**
Ruedi Wegmann

**URL**
www.callyouback.ch

**COUNTRY**
Switzerland

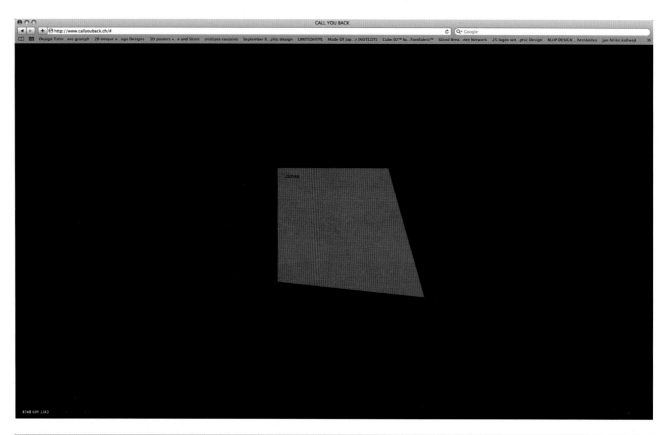

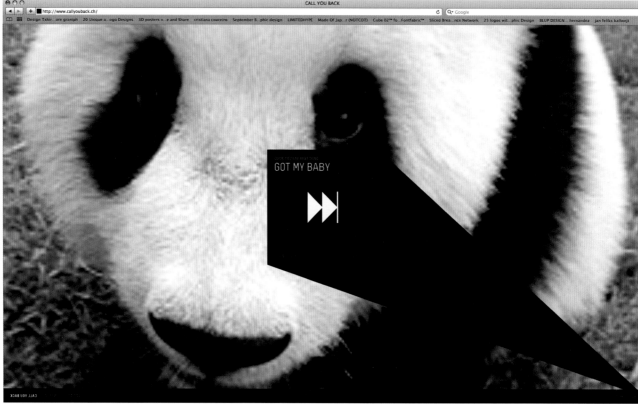

Call you back is simple and to the point: it promotes the band's music while also appropriately reflecting this moment in visual culture. It doesn't generate new images, but uses elements of the existing visual landscape to comment on the music.

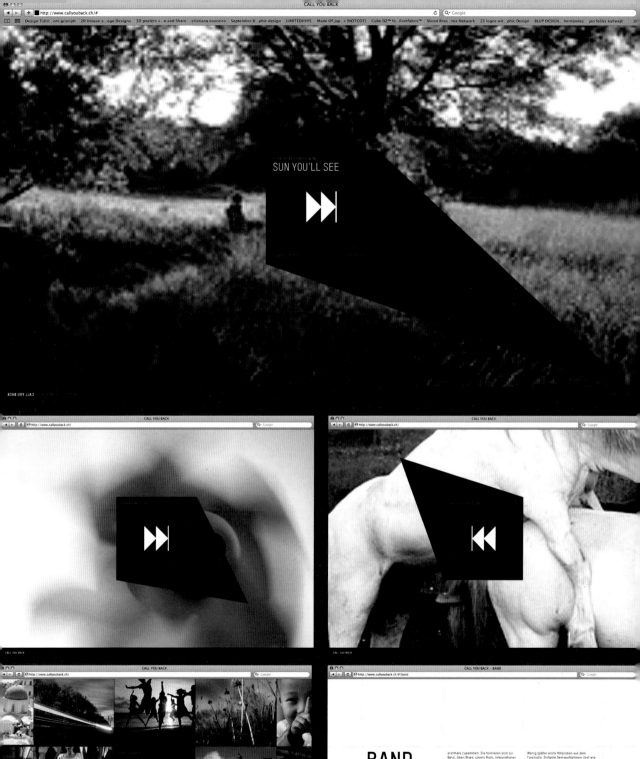

SUN YOU'LL SEE

# BAND

Guitar, Bass, Drums. Die junge Zürcher Band Call You Back ist, was lange vor ihrer Zeit entstand: ein Power-Trio, das Line-up und die Spielweise, wie sie von Cream und The Jimi Hendrix Experience begründet wurden.

Aaron Wegmann, Pascal Ammann und Dominic Eschmann, Schüler am K+S Gymnasium und Musikstudenten an der Zürcher Hochschule der Künste, spielten 2007 in einem Workshop

erstmals zusammen. Sie formieren sich zur Band, üben Blues, covern Rock, interpretieren Folk, experimentieren mit Balladen. Ein improvisiertes Clubkonzert, Anmeldung zum Nachwuchsband-Wettbewerb Band-it. Jetzt braucht's eigene Songs.

Puls, Dynamik, Muster und Strukturen, die von innen kommen, Sicherheit und Freiheit geben: Spielraum. Treibende Riffs und präzise Breaks, virtuose Linien und vage Fragmente. Jazzige und funkige Grooves, einmal mehr Jam, einmal mehr Pop. Im August 2008 stehen die drei - noch unter dem Namen Detrimentos - plötzlich auf einer grossen Bühne und ge-winnen an den Winterthurer Musikfestwochen das Band-it-Finale.

Wenig später erste Hörproben aus dem Tonstudio. Einfache Demoaufnahmen, fast wie live eingespielt und roh belassen: Crooked Smile, Slow Train, Summer. Neue Anregungen, neue Erfahrungen, neue Ideen. Was macht ein Power Trio in Zukunft? Call You Back.

AARON WEGMANN
DOMINIC ESCHMANN
PASCAL AMMANN

Download Presskit

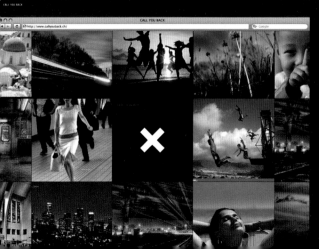

## SILVER
PROMOTIONAL SITE

**TITLE**
WWF Urwaldriese
**COMPANY**
zweipol GmbH
**CLIENT**
WWF Deutschland
**DESIGNERS**
Romana Arragone
Florian Seliger
**ART DIRECTOR**
Maik Burdina
**CREATIVE DIRECTOR**
Lucien Coy
**FLASH DEVELOPER**
Sebastian Telschow
**URL**
www.wwf.de/urwaldriese/
**COUNTRY**
Germany

**TITLE**
Dawn
**COMPANY**
Momkai
**CLIENT**
Dawn
**DESIGNER**
Harald Dunnink
Martijn
**ART DIRECTOR**
Harald Dunnink
**CREATIVE DIRECTOR**
Harald Dunnink
**URL**
www.dawn.nl
**COUNTRY**
The Netherlands

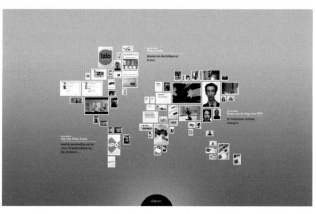

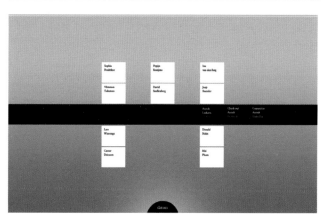

# SILVER
## PROMOTIONAL SITE

**TITLE**
Yello
**COMPANY**
Hinderling Volkart Web Identity
**CLIENT**
Yello
**DESIGNER**
Iwan Negro
**ART DIRECTORS**
Iwan Negro
Michael Hinderling
**CREATIVE DIRECTOR**
Michael Hinderling
**PHOTOGRAPHER**
Kevin Blanc
**URL**
www.yello.com
**COUNTRY**
Switzerland

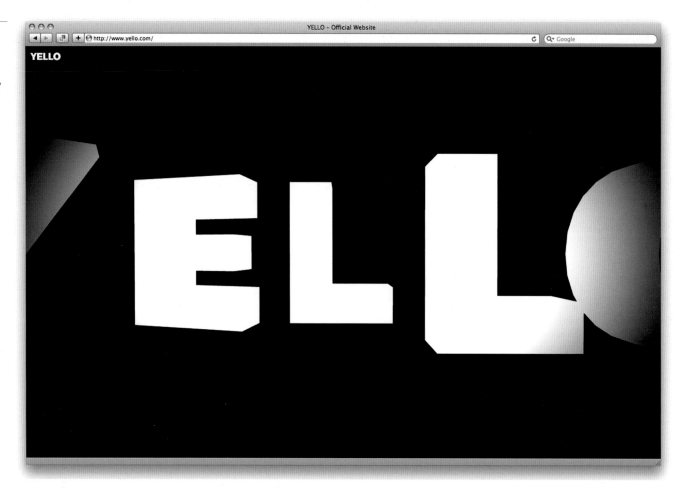

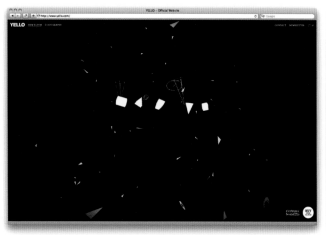

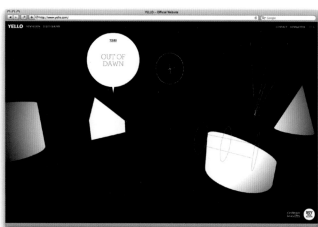

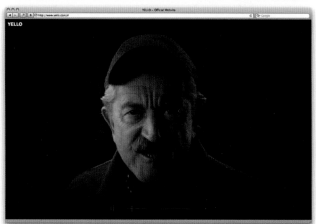

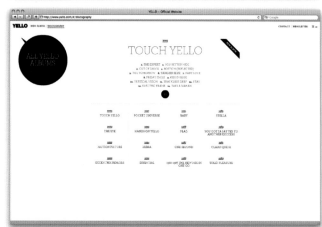

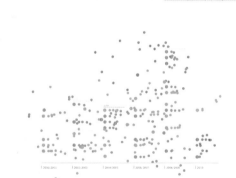

# BRONZE
## PROMOTIONAL SITE

**TITLE**
HEWI Corporate Website for
an architectural system supplier
**COMPANY**
Markwald und Neusitzer
Kommunikationsdesign GbR
**CLIENT**
HEWI Heinrich Wilke GmbH
**URL**
www.hewi.com
**COUNTRY**
Germany

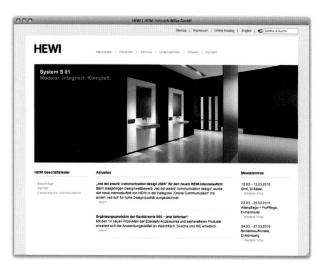

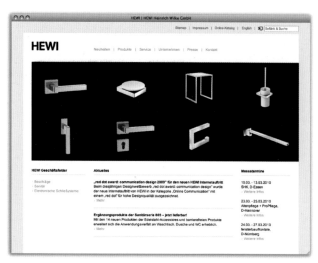

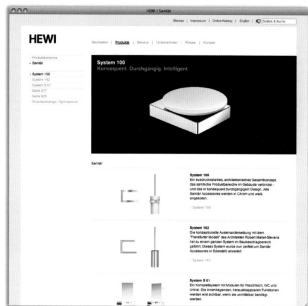

**TITLE**
ansagetext.at
**COMPANY**
Linie 3 - Design
& Werbeagentur GmbH
**CLIENT**
Florian Sekira
**URL**
www.ansagetext.at
**COUNTRY**
Austria

**TITLE**
Santa Eulalia
**COMPANY**
ESIETE
**CLIENT**
Santa Eulalia
**URL**
www.santaeulalia.com
**COUNTRY**
Spain

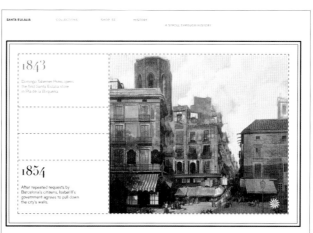

# FINALIST
## PROMOTIONAL SITE

**TITLE**
Oil Norway 40 Years
**COMPANY**
Fi
**CLIENT**
Kitchen
**URL**
www.oljenorge40ar.no
**COUNTRY**
Sweden

**TITLE**
St. Gilgen International School
**COMPANY**
wollzelle GmbH
**CLIENT**
St. Gilgen International School,
Austria
**URL**
stgis.at
**COUNTRY**
Austria

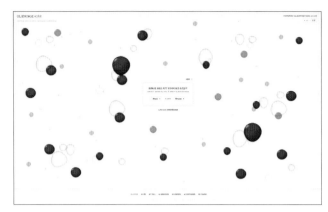

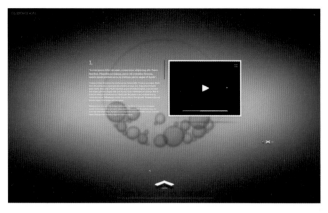

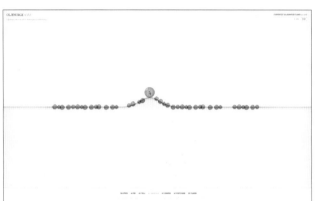

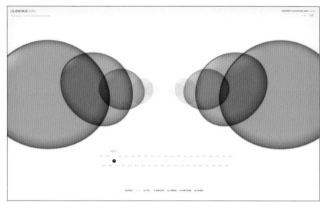

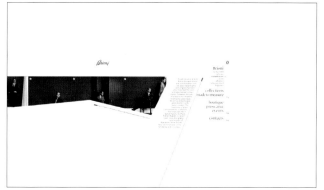

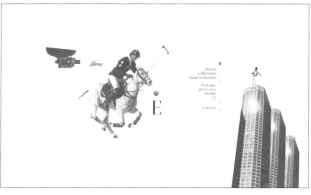

**TITLE**
Brioni
**COMPANY**
studio FM milano
**CLIENT**
Brioni
**URL**
brioni.it
**COUNTRY**
Italy

**TITLE**
www.reihenhaus.de
**COMPANY**
Die Firma GmbH
**CLIENT**
Deutsche Reihenhaus AG
**URL**
www.reihenhaus.de
**COUNTRY**
Germany

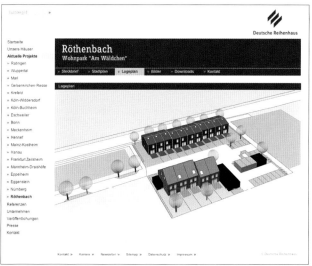

**TITLE**
Steellife
**COMPANY**
Studio Chiesa
**CLIENT**
Marcegaglia
**URL**
www.steellife.it
**COUNTRY**
Italy

**TITLE**
KHR Architects on the Move
**COMPANY**
LOOP Associates
**CLIENT**
KHR
**URL**
www.khr.dk
**COUNTRY**
Denmark

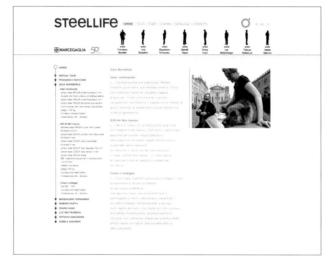

TITLE
Bad weather. Perfect day.
COMPANY
Ottoboni
CLIENT
Stadium
URL
jackor.stadium.se/en
COUNTRY
Sweden

TITLE
Karlshochschule
COMPANY
emotion effects GmbH
CLIENT
Karlshochschule Karlsruhe
URL
www.karlshochschule.de
COUNTRY
Germany

# GOLD
## INFORMATION SITE

**TITLE**
City One Minutes
**COMPANY**
Fabrique Communicatie
en Design
**CLIENT**
Holland Doc 24/VPRO and
The One Minutes Stichting
**DESIGNER**
Matthe Stet
**ART DIRECTOR**
Ronnie Besseling
**OTHER**
Emko Bos
**INTERACTION DESIGNER**
Paul Stork
**ACCOUNT TECH DIRECTOR**
Jeroen de Zwart
**PROJECT MANAGER**
Valentijn Webbers
**URL**
www.cityoneminutes.org
**COUNTRY**
The Netherlands

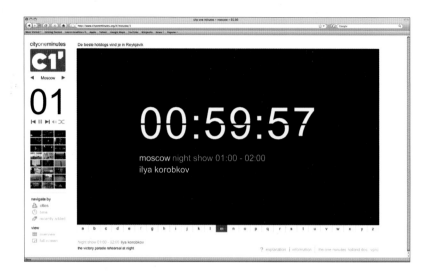

The website offers an excellent and simple user experience, where you instantly learn how to move through the video contents, accessible in different ways. It's a well-designed application that also offers great entertainment. The design is never overwhelming, and is very clever.

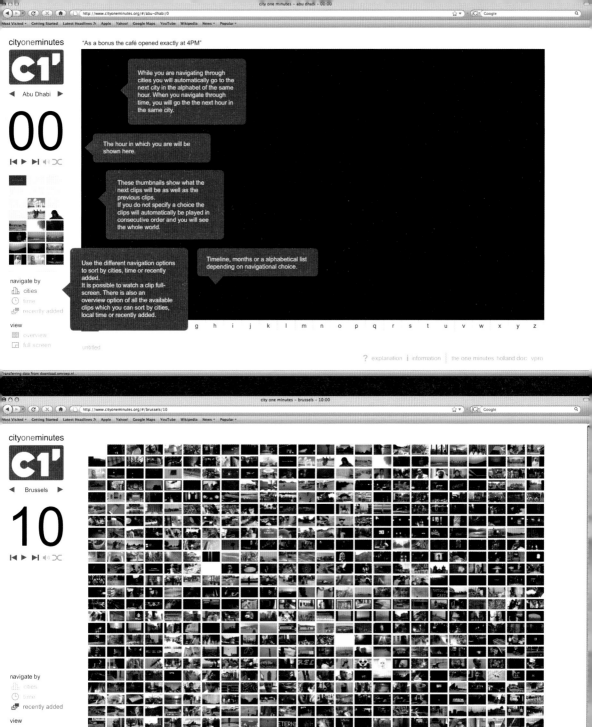

**TITLE**
Nextroom
**COMPANY**
bauer konzept
& gestaltung gmbh
**CLIENT**
nextroom
**DESIGNER**
Manuel Radde
**CREATIVE DIRECTOR**
Erwin K. Bauer
**URL**
www.nextroom.at
**COUNTRY**
Austria

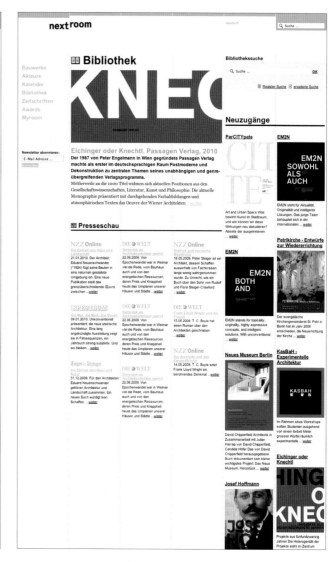

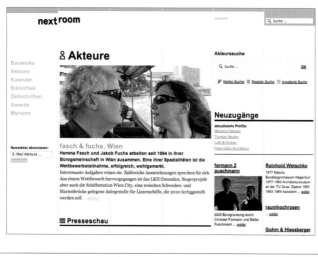

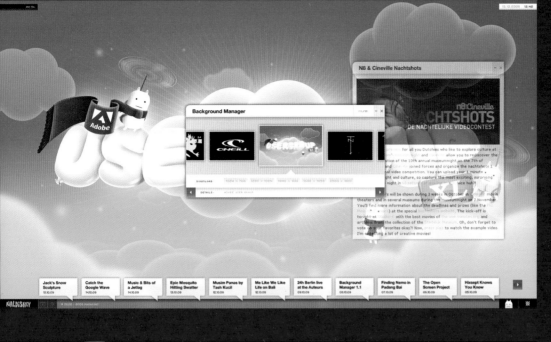

TITLE
Nalden.net
COMPANY
Momkai
CLIENT
Nalden
DESIGNER
Harald Dunnink
URL
www.nalden.net
COUNTRY
The Netherlands

## BRONZE
### INFORMATION SITE

**TITLE**
Virtuele reconstructie
Scholtenhuis
**COMPANY**
OVCG
**CLIENT**
Stichting Oorlogs -
en Verzetscentrum Groningen
(OVCG)
**URL**
www.scholtenhuis.nl
**COUNTRY**
The Netherlands

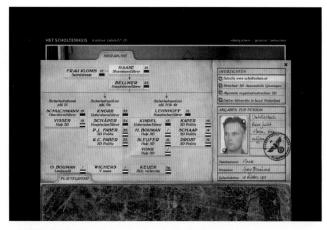

TITLE
City Portal Rotterdam
COMPANY
Mangrove
CLIENT
Rotterdam
URL
www.rotterdam.nl
COUNTRY
The Netherlands

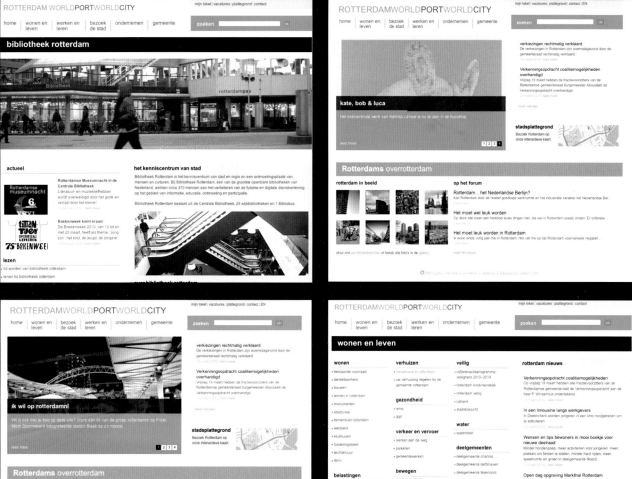

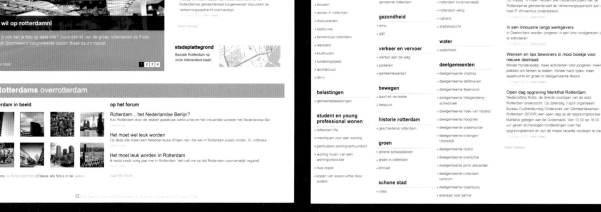

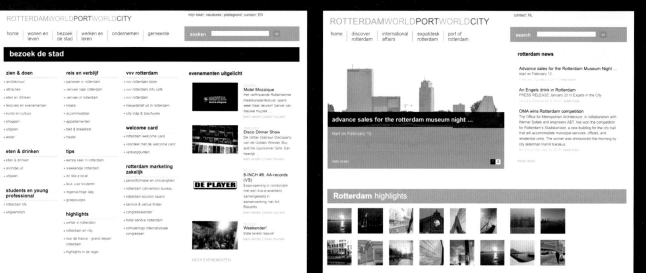

# BRONZE
INFORMATION SITE

**TITLE**
OIFF 2009
**COMPANY**
This Way Design
**CLIENT**
Oslo International Film Festival
**URL**
www.oslofilmfestival.com
**COUNTRY**
Norway

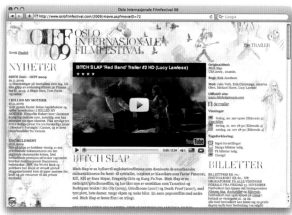

TITLE
Formex Magazine
COMPANY
Ottoboni
CLIENT
Formex
URL
www.formexmagazine.se
COUNTRY
Sweden

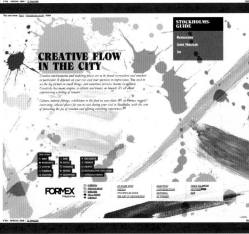

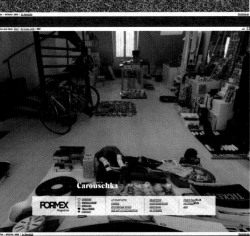

# GOLD
MOTION GRAPHICS

**TITLE**
There are more than 11 trillion
things to learn
**COMPANY**
Paul Postma
en Christian Borstlap
**CLIENT**
The Foundation for Children's
Welfare Stamps Netherlands
in collaboration with TNT Post
**ART DIRECTOR**
Christian Borstlap en Paul
Postma
**CREATIVE DIRECTOR**
Christian Borstlap
**COPYWRITER**
Christian Borstlap
**EDITOR**
Paul Postma
**ILLUSTRATOR**
Christian Borstlap
**DIRECTOR**
Paul Postma
**ANIMATION**
Paul Postma
**URL**
www.motiondesign.nl/#/motion/
showreel/kinderpostzegels2009/
**COUNTRY**
The Netherlands

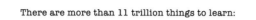

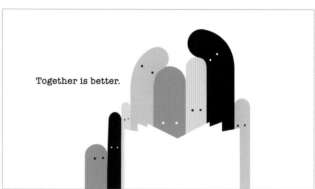

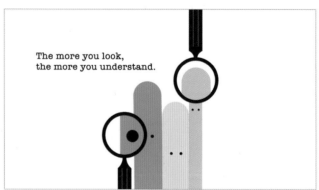

This project succeeds in making characters out of simple forms,
using graphics that are appropriate to both children and adults. It
has an excellent visual translation of contents. And it's fun!

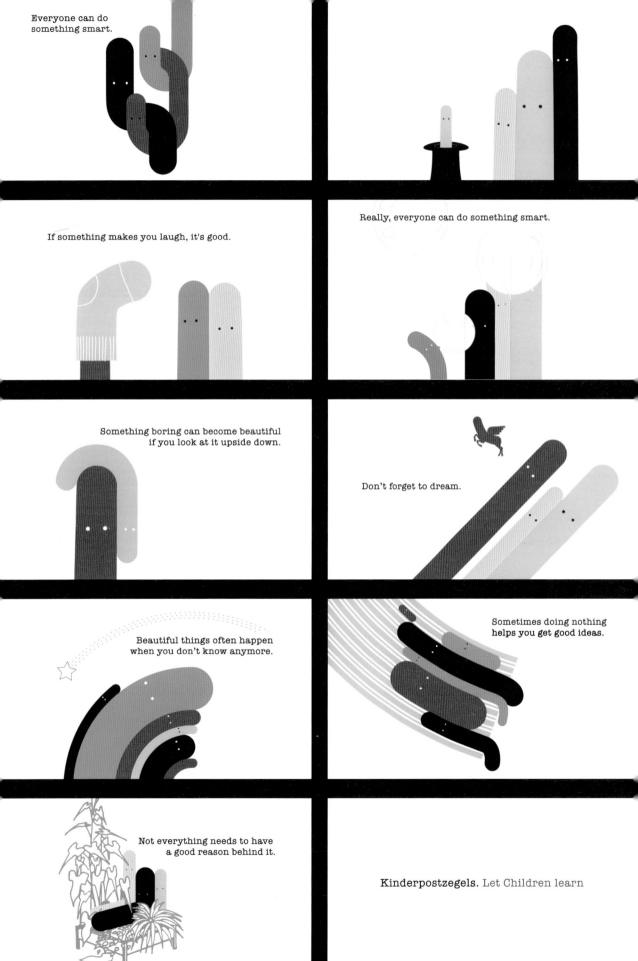

Everyone can do
something smart.

If something makes you laugh, it's good.

Really, everyone can do something smart.

Something boring can become beautiful
if you look at it upside down.

Don't forget to dream.

Beautiful things often happen
when you don't know anymore.

Sometimes doing nothing
helps you get good ideas.

Not everything needs to have
a good reason behind it.

**Kinderpostzegels.** Let Children learn

# SILVER
## MOTION GRAPHICS

**TITLE**
The Big Bank Theory
**COMPANY**
Postma | Graphics and Motion
**CLIENT**
Alex Bank
**ART DIRECTORS**
Raoul Deleo
Paul Postma
**CREATIVE DIRECTOR**
Paul Postma
**COPYWRITERS**
David Snellenberg
Dawn
**EDITOR**
The Embassadors
**ILLUSTRATOR**
Raoul Deleo
**DIRECTOR**
Paul Postma
**URL**
www.motiondesign.nl/#/motion/
showreel/alexcommercial/
**COUNTRY**
The Netherlands

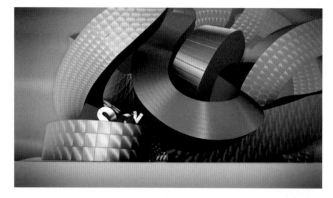
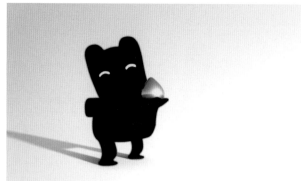

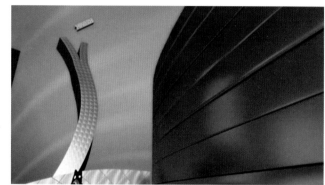
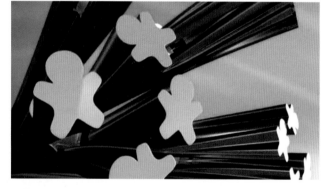

## SILVER
### MOTION GRAPHICS

TITLE
Pimp My Planet
COMPANY
Studio Smack
CLIENT
Stichting KOP & Stichting MU
DESIGNERS
Ton Meijdam
Thom Snels
Bela Zsigmond
EDITORS
Ton Meijdam
Thom Snels
Bela Zsigmond
URL
www.studiosmack.
nl/#pimpmyplanet
COUNTRY
The Netherlands

# BRONZE
## MOTION GRAPHICS

**TITLE**
Urban Abstract
**COMPANY**
Musuta Ltd.
**CLIENT**
Sanoma Television Oy Nelonen
**URL**
urban-abstract.com
**COUNTRY**
Finland

**TITLE**
Marsheaux
**COMPANY**
Beetroot Design Group
**CLIENT**
Marsheaux
**URL**
vimeo.com/9328995
**COUNTRY**
Greece

**TITLE**
Barcelona Turns Around Design
**COMPANY**
ESIETE
**CLIENT**
BCD Barcelona Centre Disseny
**URL**
www.barcelonadesignweek.es
**COUNTRY**
Spain

**FINALIST**
MOTION GRAPHICS

TITLE
OPAP - Invisible Players
COMPANY
nomint
CLIENT
OPAP
URL
www.nomint.gr/#/Work/
Eurobasket___2009/
COUNTRY
Greece

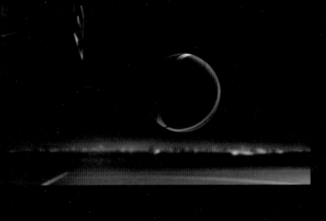

## GOLD
MISCELLANEOUS
DIGITAL MEDIA

**TITLE**
Bubole - interactive
computers game
**COMPANY**
Hipopotam studio
**DESIGNERS**
Aleksandra and Daniel
Mizielińscy
**URL**
www.bubole.pl
**COUNTRY**
Poland

Character design is the strongest point in this project, but all the visual elements, with the help of an excellently integrated sound, visuals and action, contribute to create an enjoyable experience. Even if the game in itself is a very simple one, it's involving and funny, and has a clever way of displaying the users that are online at the same time.

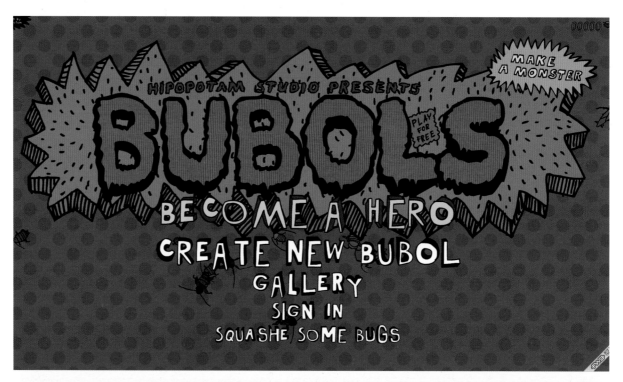

**TITLE**
Inostudio Inform 2.0
**COMPANY**
Design Aspekt
**CLIENT**
Inostudio
**DESIGNERS**
Martina Grabovszky
Michael Schmidt
**ART DIRECTOR**
Martina Grabovszky
**CREATIVE DIRECTOR**
Christian Riss
**URL**
www.inostudio.de/downloads/
inform.zip
**COUNTRY**
Germany

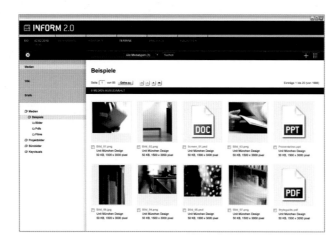

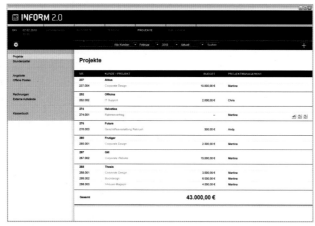

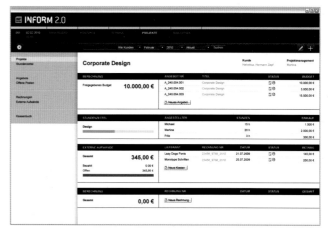

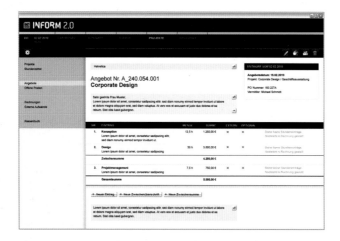

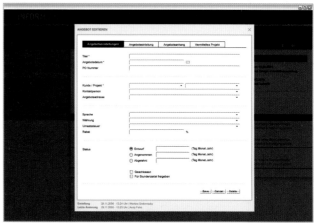

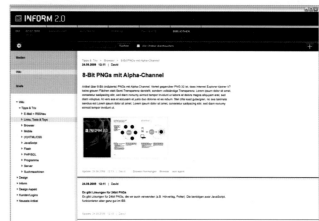

TITLE
HoodooVoodoo
COMPANY
Visualizers
CLIENT
Cuberoom
URL
visualizers.com.ua/apps/
hoodoovoodoo/
COUNTRY
Ukraine

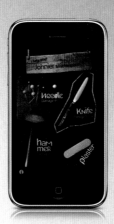

Are you an angel? Do you like all of the people around?! Then you won't need this Hoodoo doll! But... You aren't an angel. Do some calls from your contacts bore or disturb you? Did your boss put out on you? Are you depressed? Voodoo is right choice!

www.cuberoom.biz/apps/hoodoo

 http://itunes.apple.com/WebObjects/MZStore.woa/wa/viewSoftware?id=320131074&mt=8

TITLE
Adobe User Group identity
COMPANY
Momkai
CLIENT
Adobe User Group
URL
www.adobeusergroup.nl
COUNTRY
Netherlands

## FINALIST
### MISCELLANEOUS DIGITAL MEDIA

**TITLE**
Information Centre Delft Bouwt
**COMPANY**
MCW Studio's
**CLIENT**
Gemeente Delft / Bliksems
**COUNTRY**
The Netherlands

PACKAGING

# GOLD
PACKAGING
ALCOHOLIC DRINKS

**TITLE**
2010
**COMPANY**
Bendita Gloria
**CLIENT**
Casa Mariol
**COUNTRY**
Spain

Casa Mariol is an organic wine company, and the design of this "special edition" wine respects the principles of essentiality and minimum intervention on the product. With this design solution, the receiver of this gift gets a personal message, that goes beyond the normal function of a label to become a poster, while leaving the bottle untouched and perfectly reusable.

# BRONZE
PACKAGING
ALCOHOLIC DRINKS

**TITLE**
Naked King
**COMPANY**
Beetroot Design Group
**CLIENT**
Argyropoulos/Pieria Eratini
Estate
**COUNTRY**
Greece

**TITLE**
Lo Mon
**COMPANY**
ruiz+company
**CLIENT**
Trossos del Priorat
**COUNTRY**
Spain

**TITLE**
Tatranský čaj - Tatratea
**COMPANY**
KARLOFF s. r. o.
**CLIENT**
Karloff
**COUNTRY**
Slovakia

**FINALIST**
PACKAGING
ALCOHOLIC DRINKS

**TITLE**
Blossa 09
**COMPANY**
BVD.
Blidholm Vagnemark Design
**CLIENT**
Pernod Ricard Sweden
**COUNTRY**
Sweden

# GOLD
PACKAGING
FOOD & BEVERAGES

**TITLE**
Økologisk steinbakt mel
**COMPANY**
Strømme Throndsen Design
**CLIENT**
Holli Mølle
**DESIGNER**
Eia Grødal
**CREATIVE DIRECTOR**
Morten Throndsen
**COUNTRY**
Norway

A simple design that is appropriate to the product and developed in an intelligent way, optimising the production process: the main part of the package remains the same, while the colour coded stripes identify the different kinds of flour.

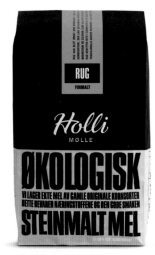 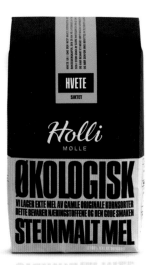   

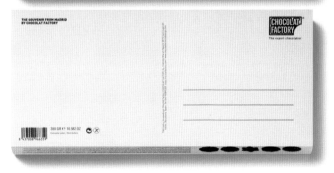

**TITLE**
The Souvenirs
**COMPANY**
ruiz+company
**CLIENT**
Chocolat Factory
**DESIGNER**
Vicente Ruiz
**ART DIRECTOR**
Ainhoa Nagore
**CREATIVE DIRECTOR**
David Ruiz
**COPYWRITER**
Jorge Alavedra
**COUNTRY**
Spain

# BRONZE
PACKAGING
FOOD & BEVERAGES

**TITLE**
Sugarillos Sugar Sticks
**COMPANY**
Mousegraphics
**CLIENT**
Sugarillos S.A.
**COUNTRY**
Greece

**TITLE**
Skinka frå Suldal
**COMPANY**
fasett
**CLIENT**
Energihotellet
**URL**
www.skinka.no
**COUNTRY**
Norway

# BRONZE
## PACKAGING
## FOOD & BEVERAGES

**TITLE**
Caffè Fresko
**COMPANY**
Alessandro Costariol
**CLIENT**
Santos Caffè E Affini S.R.L.
**COUNTRY**
Italy

## FINALIST
PACKAGING
FOOD & BEVERAGES

**TITLE**
mastihashop - chocolate rounds
**COMPANY**
Looking Agency S.A
**CLIENT**
mastihashop
**COUNTRY**
Greece

**TITLE**
ChariTea
**COMPANY**
BVD.
Blidholm Vagnemark Design
**CLIENT**
LemonAid Beverages GmbH
**COUNTRY**
Sweden

**TITLE**
Willie's Supreme
& Delectable Cacao
**COMPANY**
Taxi Studio
**CLIENT**
El Tesoro
**COUNTRY**
United Kingdom

# SILVER
## PACKAGING
## MISCELLANIOUS

**TITLE**
Helgo ABC Friendly,
Cool and Warm
**COMPANY**
LOOP Associates
**CLIENT**
Helgo ABC
**CREATIVE DIRECTOR**
Peter van Toorn Brix
**COUNTRY**
Denmark

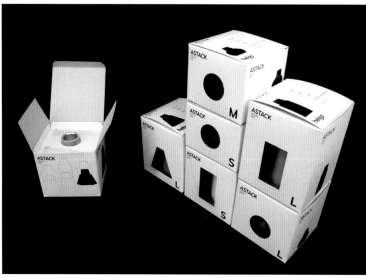

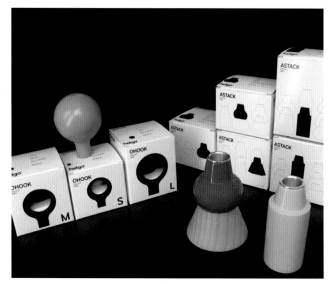

**TITLE**
Express
**COMPANY**
Dimopoulos Karatzas
**CLIENT**
Apivita
**DESIGNERS**
Petros Dimopoulos
John Karatzas
Konstantina Vezou
**CREATIVE DIRECTOR**
Petros Dimopoulos
**ILLUSTRATOR**
Vasilis Gousis
**COUNTRY**
Greece

**TITLE**
Laid
**COMPANY**
Skin Design AS
**CLIENT**
Laid Ltd
**DESIGNER**
Skin Designstudio
**COUNTRY**
Norway

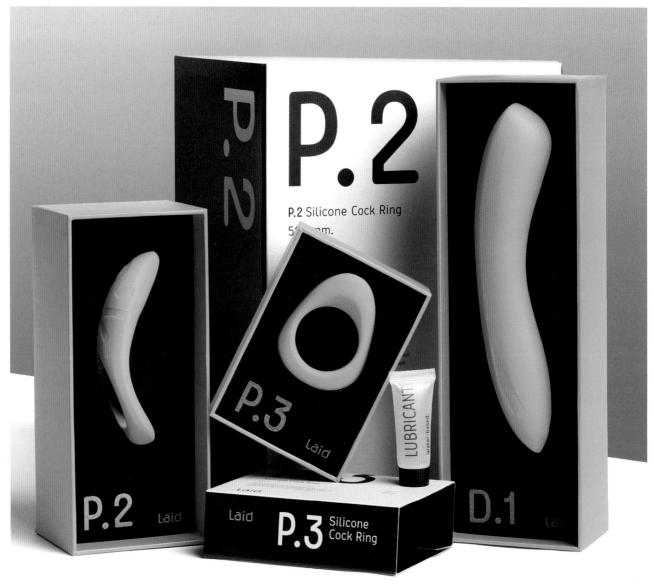

**TITLE**
WOW
**COMPANY**
merkwürdig gmbh
**CLIENT**
Bailly Diehl
**DESIGNERS**
Nadine Häfner
Jennifer Staudacher
Kai Staudacher
**COUNTRY**
Germany

**TITLE**
Ivancic I Sinovi
Packaging System
**COMPANY**
SVIDesign
**CLIENT**
Ivancic I Sinovi
**DESIGNERS**
Sasha Vidakovic
Ian Mizon
**ART DIRECTOR**
Sasha Vidakovic
**CREATIVE DIRECTOR**
Sasha Vidakovic
**ILLUSTRATORS**
Sasha Vidakovic
Ian Mizon
**COUNTRY**
United Kingdom

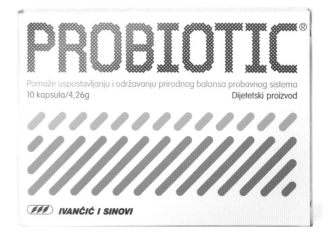

**BRONZE**
PACKAGING
MISCELLANIOUS

**TITLE**
Petrocoll Spatula Putty
**COMPANY**
Mousegraphics
**CLIENT**
Petrocoll S.A.
**COUNTRY**
Greece

**TITLE**
Men's care
**COMPANY**
Dimopoulos Karatzas
**CLIENT**
Apivita
**COUNTRY**
Greece

**FINALIST**
PACKAGING
MISCELLANIOUS

**TITLE**
Grow Your Own
**COMPANY**
Turner Duckworth:
London & San Francisco
**CLIENT**
Homebase
**COUNTRY**
United Kingdom

**TITLE**
Monoprix Birthday Party
**COMPANY**
Les Bons Faiseurs
**CLIENT**
Monoprix
**COUNTRY**
France

# GOLD
CD/DVD COVER

**TITLE**
Elyjah: Planet, Planet.
**COMPANY**
Zwölf
**CLIENT**
Klimbim Records
**DESIGNERS**
Stefan Guzy
Björn Wiede
**PHOTOGRAPHER**
Norman Konrad
**PRODUCER**
Markus Lisse
**PRINTERS**
Museum Kreuzberg
**COUNTRY**
Germany

The design conveys in an unusual way the atmosphere connected to the music. The cover is a physical object that creates a connection between the listener and the music. The uniqueness of each copy gives fans a strong reason to buy the record.

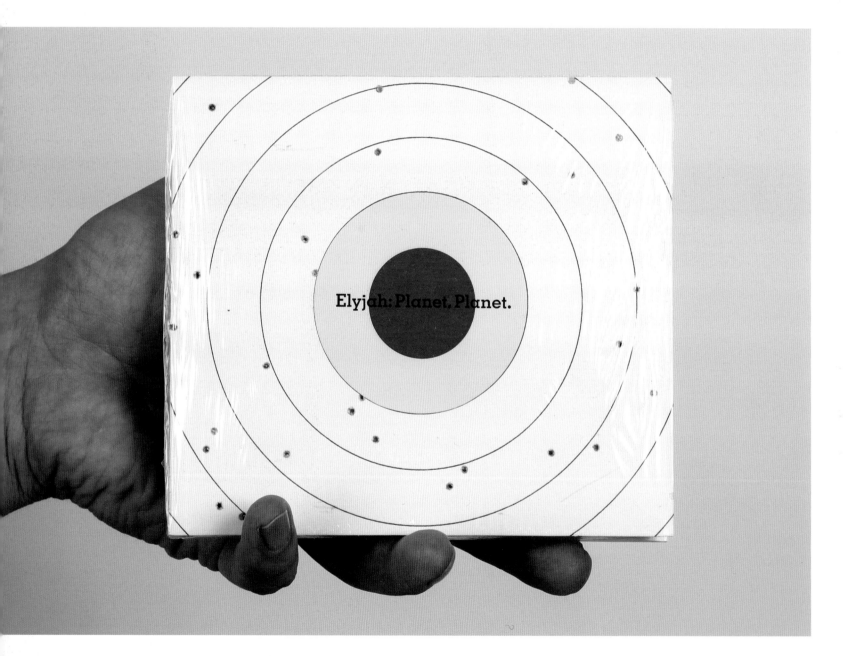

TITLE
Legends of Benin
COMPANY
Sosumi
CLIENT
Analog Africa
DESIGNERS
Petra Schröder
Dirk von Manteuffel
ART DIRECTORS
Petra Schröder
Dirk von Manteuffel
CREATIVE DIRECTORS
Petra Schröder
Dirk von Manteuffel
COUNTRY
Germany

# SILVER
## CD/DVD COVER

**TITLE**
Ensemble Modern Portrait CD
**COMPANY**
Jäger & Jäger
**CLIENT**
Ensemble Modern
**CREATIVE DIRECTORS**
Regina Jäger
Olaf Jäger
**PHOTOGRAPHER**
Olaf Jäger
**COUNTRY**
Germany

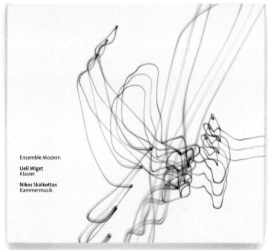

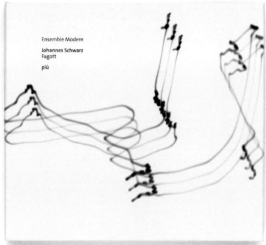

**TITLE**
Electronically Yours
**COMPANY**
mnp
**CLIENT**
Undo records
**COUNTRY**
Greece

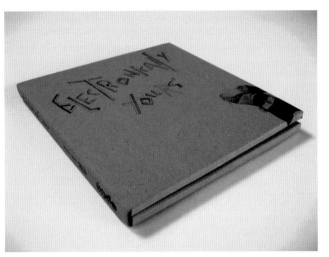

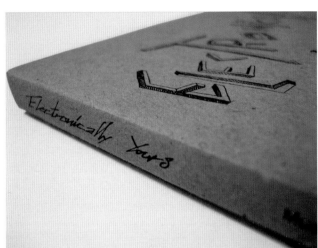

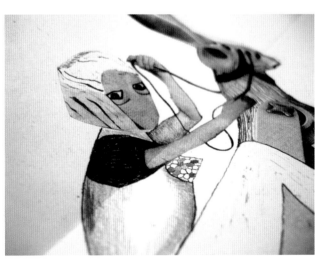

# BRONZE
CD/DVD COVER

**TITLE**
Lars Winnerback box
**COMPANY**
HFDP
**CLIENT**
Universal Music Sweden
**COUNTRY**
Sweden

**BRONZE**
CD/DVD COVER

**TITLE**
Antonioni DVDbox
**COMPANY**
rrdesign
**CLIENT**
GUTEK FILM
**COUNTRY**
Poland

**TITLE**
School Film Library
**COMPANY**
Monika Zawadzki
**CLIENT**
Polish Film Institute and
Polish Audiovisual Institute.
**COUNTRY**
Poland

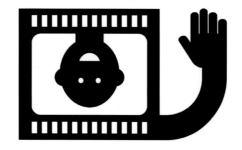

# Filmoteka
# Szkolna

ZEZOWATE SZCZĘŚCIE
**F O T E L**

SÓL ZIEMI CZARNEJ
**JESTEM ZŁY**

**D Ł U G**
**NASZA ULICA**

**HYDROZAGADKA**
POLSKA KRONIKA NON CAMEROWA NR-1

**ABEL, TWÓJ BRAT**
**MĘSKA SPRAWA**

UCIECZKA Z KINA „WOLNOŚĆ"
**E X I T**

**E R O I C A**
OSTRY FILM ZAANGAŻOWANY

**A M A T O R**
ĆWICZENIA WARSZTATOWE

**NIENORMALNI**
Z PUNKTU WIDZENIA NOCNEGO PORTIERA

**ARIA DLA ATLETY**
**DZIEWCZYNY DO WZIĘCIA**

**DEJA VU**
WYJŚCIE NA JAW ROBOTNIKÓW KINA Z FABRYKI SNÓW

**BRZEZINA**
**ŁAGODNA**

STRUKTURA KRYSZTAŁU
**T A N G O**

**GRY ULICZNE**
STROJENIE INSTRUMENTÓW

**ILUMINACJA**
**PREKURSOR**

**ZMRUŻ OCZY**
**GADAJĄCE GŁOWY**

**CZEŚĆ TERESKA**
**RODZINA CZŁOWIECZA**

JAK BYĆ KOCHANĄ
**...PORTRET WŁASNY**

**FOTOAMATOR**
USŁYSZCIE MÓJ KRZYK
ŻYWOT MATEUSZA
**S C H O D Y**
**A R K A**

**POPIÓŁ I DIAMENT**
KRÓTKA HISTORIA JEDNEJ TABLICY
**C H L E B**

HISTORIA KINA W POPIELAWACH
**OCZY UROCZNE**

WSZYSTKO MOŻE SIĘ PRZYTRAFIĆ
**SZCZUROŁAP**
SIEDEM KOBIET W RÓŻNYM WIEKU

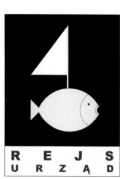

**R E J S**
**U R Z Ą D**

TITLE
The Penny Black Remedy CD
COMPANY
Laboratorium
CLIENT
The Penny Black Remedy
COUNTRY
Croatia

ILLUSTRATIONS

**TITLE**
Its cool to be five!
**COMPANY**
Iván Solbes SL
**CLIENT**
Revolution Publicidad
**DESIGNER**
Ivan Solbes
**ART DIRECTOR**
Ivan Solbes
**CREATIVE DIRECTOR**
Ivan Solbes
**COPYWRITER**
Jose Maria Mayorga & Alf Garcia
**ILLUSTRATOR**
Ivan Solbes
**COUNTRY**
Spain

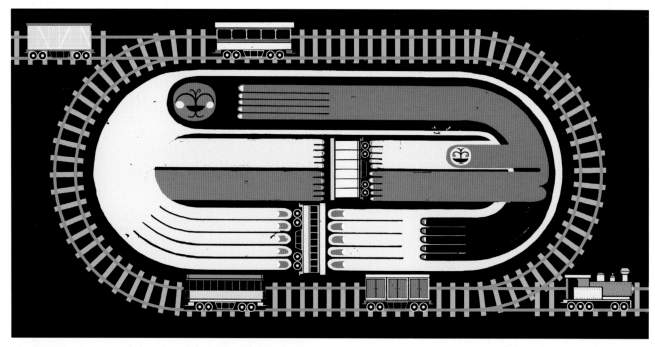

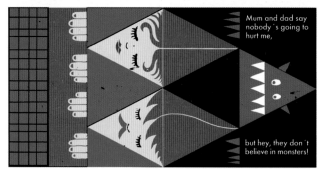

Mum and dad say
nobody´s going to
hurt me,

but hey, they don´t
believe in monsters!

I´ve found out that if I say my
belly aches when there´s
something for lunch that I don´t
like, my parents got annoyed,
but they don´t insist.

Sometimes I even think if mum and
dad would forget to come back home
one night, I could survive if my nose
keeps as productive as it is now.

The bad side is when afterwords
they catch me if I ask for
icecream. I think I should
measure out this tactic.

This illustrated book shows an unusual view on childhood, assuming a five-year old child's point of view, where everyone and everything is exaggerated. Avoiding all stereotyped imagery, the illustrations effectively use geometric shapes to convey a child's world in an almost abstract way, and are well integrated in the book form.

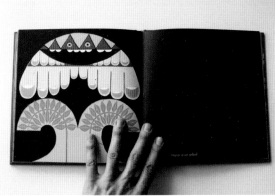

# GOLD
## BOOK & EDITORIAL ILLUSTRATION

**TITLE**
The Soul of Motown
**COMPANY**
Drushba Pankow
**CLIENT**
EMI Music Publishing Germany
GmbH, edel Germany GmbH
**DESIGNERS**
Alexandra Kardinar
Volker Schlecht
**COPYWRITER**
Torsten Gross
**EDITORS**
Constanze Goelz
Seraina Nyikos
Manuel Tessloff
**ILLUSTRATORS**
Alexandra Kardinar
Volker Schlecht
**COUNTRY**
Germany

The illustrations set a perfect background for the theme of the book, with an excellent mix of urban elements and typographic details which effectively transmit the feeling of the Motown period.

TITLE
Bitch
COMPANY
Štěpánka Bláhovcová
CLIENT
Gallery Ltd.
DESIGNERS
Štěpánka Bláhovcová
Anna Citterbardová
COPYWRITERS
Štěpánka Bláhovcová
Anna Citterbardová
Roald Dahl
Jaroslav Kořán
Gallery Ltd
ILLUSTRATOR
Štěpánka Bláhovcová
COUNTRY
Czech Republic

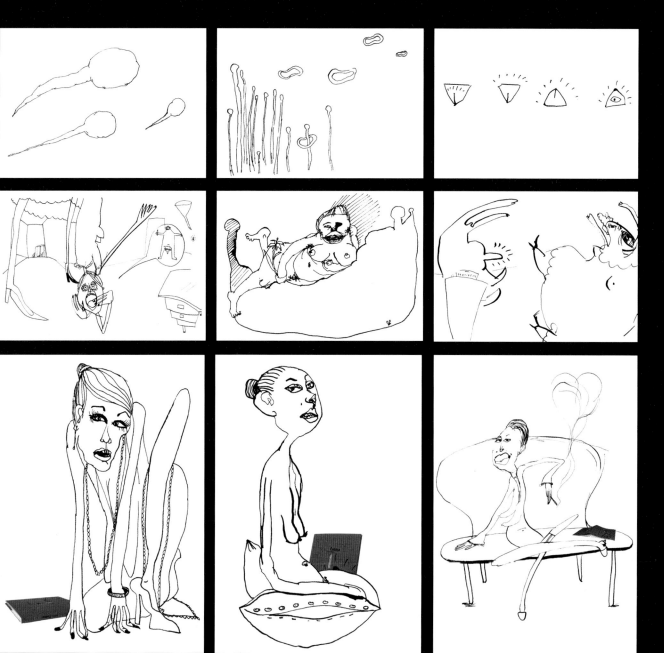

# GOLD
## CORPORATE ILLUSTRATION

**TITLE**
Torture basement
**COMPANY**
Trapped in suburbia
**CLIENT**
museumgoudA
**DESIGNERS**
Cuby Gerards
Karin Langeveld
Ulla Britt Vogt
Jordy van den Nieuwendijk
Debora Schiltmans
**ART DIRECTORS**
Cuby Gerards
Karin Langeveld
**CREATIVE DIRECTORS**
Cuby Gerards
Karin Langeveld
**COPYWRITER**
museumgoudA
**ILLUSTRATORS**
Jos Verwer
Cuby Gerards
Karin Langeveld
Ulla Britt Vogt
Jordy van den Nieuwendijk
Debora Schiltmans
**COUNTRY**
The Netherlands

The Torture basement shows a brilliant design concept based on illustration, and it perfectly addresses a clearly defined audience. The experience of visiting the museum basement with the help of a UV light becomes an adventure, and the whole space is transformed thanks to this additional layer – a true added value reached through design.

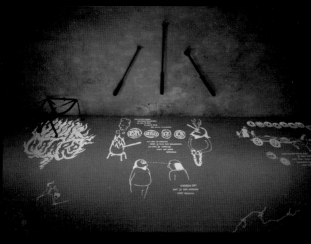

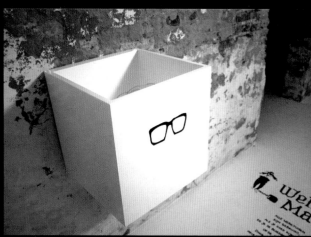

**TITLE**
Fena Spring-Summer 2009
Depth of Style
**COMPANY**
Beetroot Design Group
**CLIENT**
Fena Stores
**ART DIRECTORS**
Vagelis Liakos,
Yiannis Charalambopoulos,
Michalis Rafail,
Ilias Pantikakis
**ILLUSTRATOR**
Alexis Nikou
**COUNTRY**
Greece

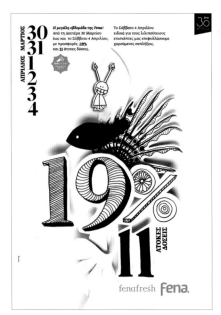

**TITLE**
trendsta
**COMPANY**
Vier für Texas
**CLIENT**
trendsta, Inc.
**URL**
www.trendsta.com
**COUNTRY**
Germany

**TITLE**
Lomography.it
**COMPANY**
Alexis Rom estudio:::
Taller Vostok
**CLIENT**
Lomographyc Society Italia
**URL**
lomography.it
**COUNTRY**
Spain

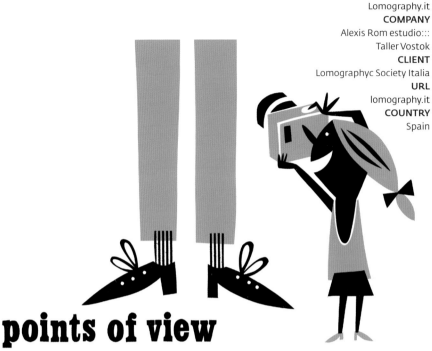

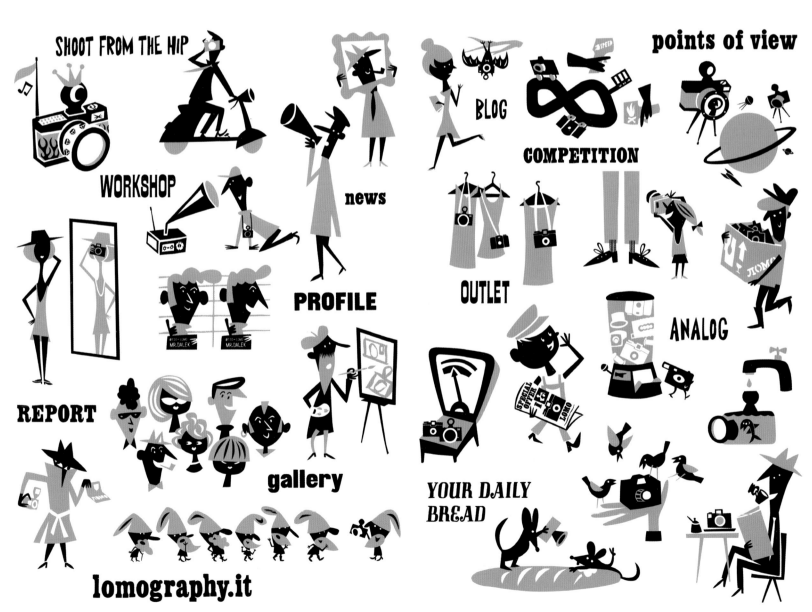

**TITLE**
In love at Carnival
**COMPANY**
polka dot design
**CLIENT**
Municipality of Xanthi
**COUNTRY**
Greece

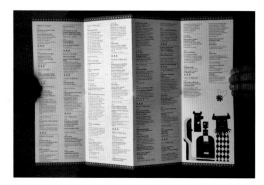

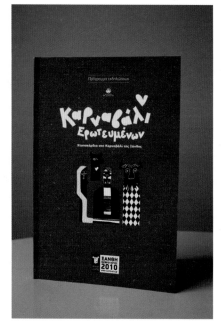

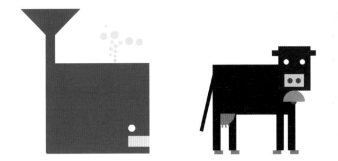

**TITLE**
Apotheek Kids
**COMPANY**
GVA Studio
**CLIENT**
Apotheek
**COUNTRY**
Switzerland

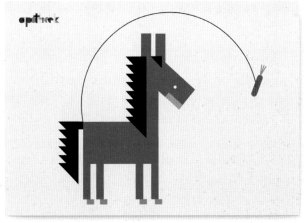

**TITLE**
"Books and more"
Papasotiriou Bookstores
**COMPANY**
designersunited.gr
**CLIENT**
Papasotiriou Bookstores
**COUNTRY**
Greece

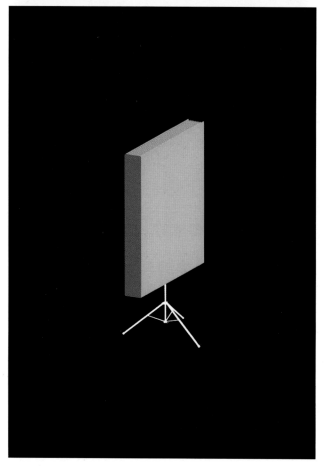

**TITLE**
Fena Fall-Winter
2009-2010 Retro
**COMPANY**
Beetroot Design Group
**CLIENT**
Fena Stores
**COUNTRY**
Greece

SELF PROMOTION

**TITLE**
Typographic Entomology
**COMPANY**
Studio FM milano srl
**COUNTRY**
Italy

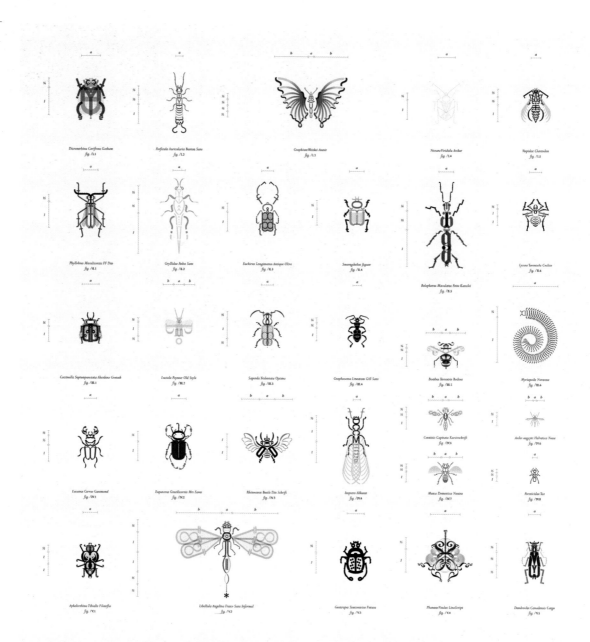

The obsessive approach chosen by Studio FM Milano for this poster says a lot about the dedication they have to design. Using entomology as a metaphor, they create a universe of typefaces classified as insects, thus revealing the unexpected potential hidden in each font. The poster is delicately designed, with an attention to tiny details and printing techniques, and proves to be a well thought-out promotion of the studio's design approach.

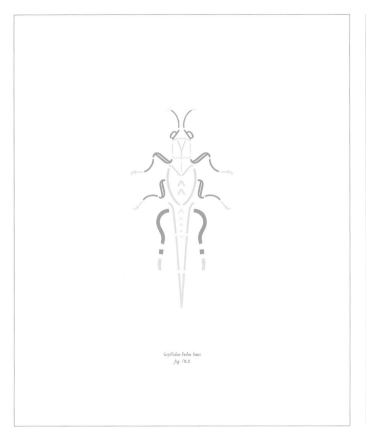

Gryllidae Indra Sans
fig. /II.2

Rhinoceros Beetle Dax Schrift
fig. /IV.3

Dicronorhina Carifrons Gotham
fig. /IV.1

Lucanus Carvus Garamond
fig. /IV.1

# SILVER
## PRINTED SELF PROMOTION

**TITLE**
Christmas Self-Promotion
**COMPANY**
Delikatessen Agentur fuer
Marken und Design GmbH
**DESIGNERS**
Trudi Steinbuss
Jesco Schoen
**CREATIVE DIRECTOR**
Robert Neumann
**COPYWRITER**
Kevin Bauer
**COUNTRY**
Germany

**TITLE**
ruiz+company
**COMPANY**
ruiz+company
**DESIGNER**
Ainhoa Nagore
**ART DIRECTOR**
Ainhoa Nagore
**CREATIVE DIRECTOR**
David Ruiz
**COUNTRY**
Spain

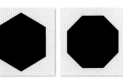
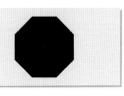
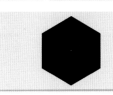

# FINALIST
PRINTED SELF PROMOTION

**TITLE**
Turner Duckworth
Holiday Card 2009
**COMPANY**
Turner Duckworth:
London & San Francisco
**COUNTRY**
United Kingdom

**TITLE**
9 Questions
**COMPANY**
Boutique Creativa
**COUNTRY**
Italy

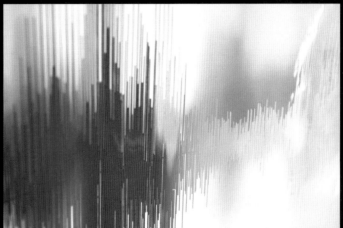

TITLE
buonduemiladieci
COMPANY
Jekyll & Hyde
COUNTRY
Italy

TITLE
Periodic Table of Time
COMPANY
Laboratorium
COUNTRY
Croatia

The navigation and usability of this portfolio site are excellent. It's a very straightforward way to promote the Momkai's design skills with innovative and fresh web design. Honest, clear and direct.

Momkai
a digital creative agency

Creatie magazine
Issue 6

Dawn
Portfolio

Amsterdam Metropolitan Area
Experience

Peugeot
Auto van 3008

Ministry of Social Affairs
Taskforce DeeltijdPlus

They
Portfolio

Nalden.net
Influential blog

Adobe User Group
Visual identity

The Netherlands Royal Air Force
Base-X

Amnesty International
Against Discrimination

Software inc.
Box covers

Veronica
Storycatcher game

Momkai
a digital creative agency

×

**TITLE**
BB (Bisgràfic Blog)
**COMPANY**
Bisgrafic
**URL**
www.bisgrafic.info
**COUNTRY**
Spain

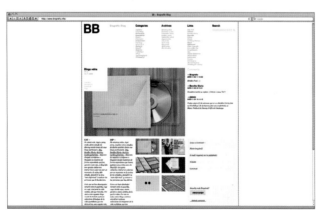

**TITLE**
aeraki.gr
**COMPANY**
aeraki
**DESIGNER**
Despina Aeraki
**COPYWRITER**
Yiannis Tsortanidis
**PHOTOGRAPHERS**
Christos Christopoulos
Despina Aeraki
**ACTION SCRIPT**
Danae Stamataki
**MUSIC**
Thodoris Forozis
**URL**
www.aeraki.gr
**COUNTRY**
Greece

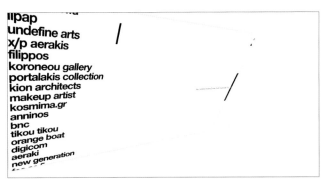

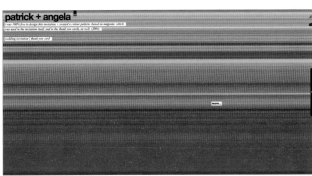

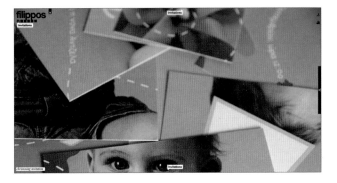

# BRONZE
DIGITAL SELF PROMOTION

**TITLE**
bleed.no
**COMPANY**
bleed
**URL**
www.bleed.no
**COUNTRY**
Norway

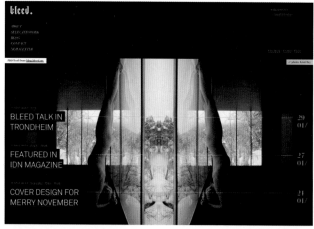

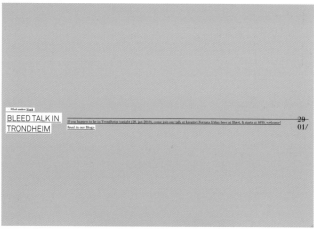

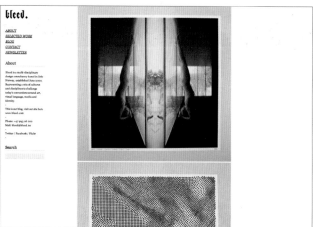

**TITLE**
www.designersunited.gr
**COMPANY**
designersunited.gr
**URL**
www.designersunited.gr
**COUNTRY**
Greece

I/DONT
THINK/THAT
NON-OBJECTIVE
FORM/IS/THE
FINAL/FORM:
IT/IS/THE
REVOLUTIONARY
CONDITION
OF/FORM

ПОСТАНОВКА

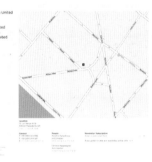

The Body Shop
Apivita
Thierry Mugler
Jo Malone
Chanel
Molton Brown

disco
ball

# FINALIST
DIGITAL SELF PROMOTION

**TITLE**
Dolphins online
**COMPANY**
Dolphins // communication design
**URL**
www.dolphinsonline.gr
**COUNTRY**
Greece

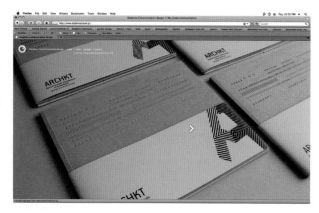

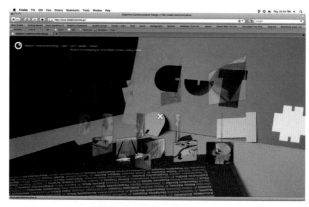
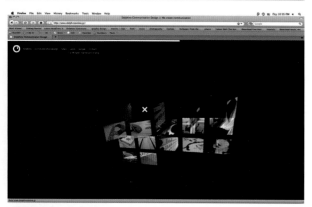

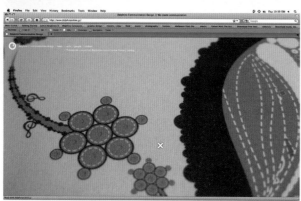
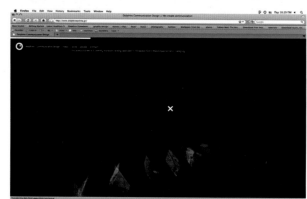

**TITLE**
www.kvorning.com
Designs in focus
**COMPANY**
Kvorning Design
& Communication
**URL**
www.kvorning.com
**COUNTRY**
Denmark

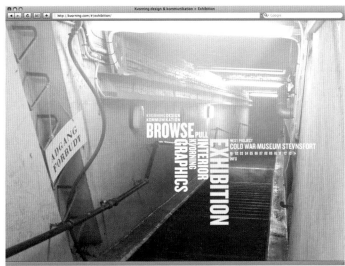

**TITLE**
Spamghetto
**COMPANY**
ToDo
**CLIENT**
self-initiated
**DESIGNERS**
Giorgio Olivero
Fabio Cionini
Fabio Franchino
Andrea Clemente
Andrea Pinchi
Riccardo Mongelluzzo
Elena Fonti
Carlo Syed
**CREATIVE DIRECTOR**
Giorgio Olivero
**URL**
www.todo.to.it/#projects/
spamghetto
**COUNTRY**
Italy

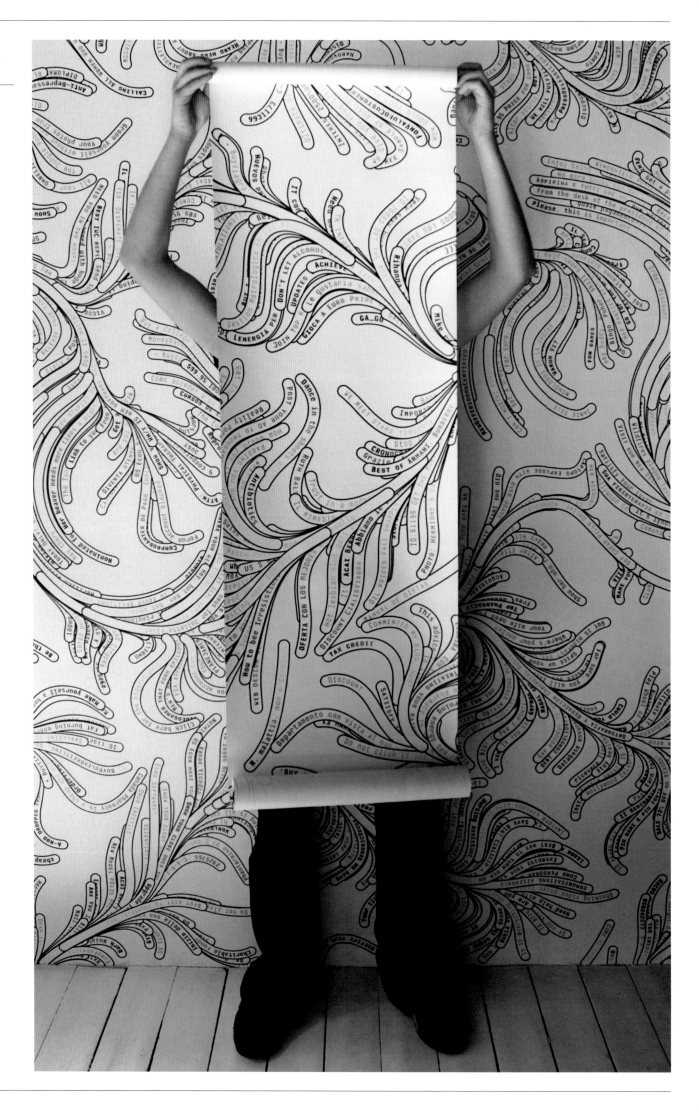

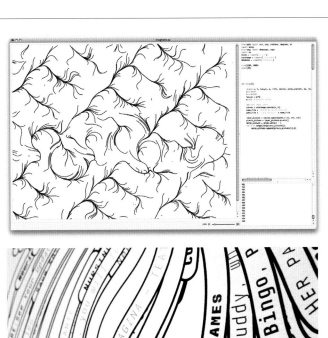
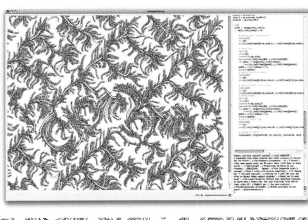
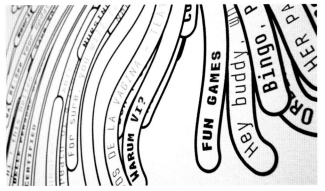

# BRONZE
SELF INITIATED PROJECTS

**TITLE**
Romeo & Juliet
**COMPANY**
Beetroot Design Group
**CLIENT**
Beetroot Design Group
**COUNTRY**
Greece

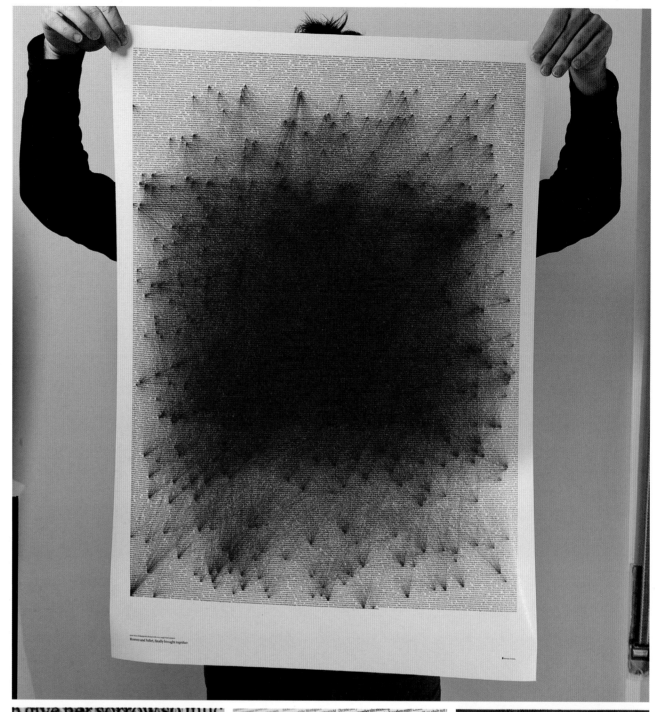

**TITLE**
exhibition
»alphabet innsbruck«
**COMPANY**
Buero Uebele Visuelle
Kommunikation
**CLIENT**
Andreas Uebele
**COUNTRY**
Germany

# BRONZE
SELF INITIATED PROJECTS

**TITLE**
Generous Gesture
**COMPANY**
Buro Petr van Blokland
+ Claudia Mens
**URL**
www.generousgesture.com
**COUNTRY**
Netherlands

**TITLE**
Keywords 1
**COMPANY**
busybuilding
**COUNTRY**
Greece

# BRONZE
SELF INITIATED PROJECTS

**TITLE**
Dollars and Roses
**COMPANY**
Gruppa Krovi
**URL**
www.gruppakrovi.com/
dollarsrozes
**COUNTRY**
Russia

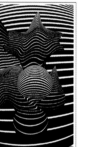

**TITLE**
Keywords2
**COMPANY**
busybuilding
**COUNTRY**
Greece

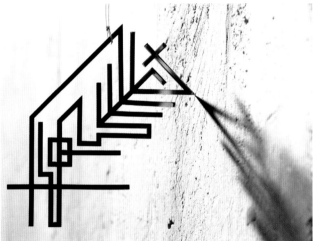

**TITLE**
Ekspektatywa (1-6)
**COMPANY**
Fundacja Nowej Kultury
Bęc Zmiana
**CLIENT**
Fundacja Bęc Zmiana
**URL**
www.ekspektatywa.pl
**COUNTRY**
Poland

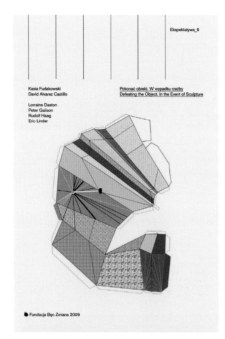

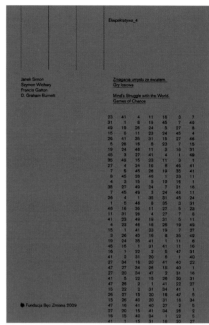

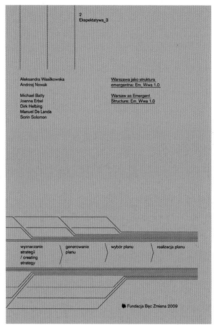

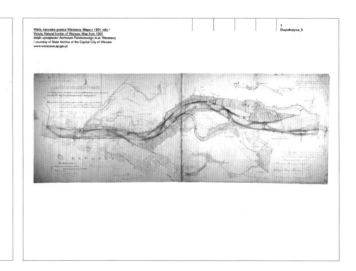

**TITLE**
FLUFF SB
**COMPANY**
vijf890
**CLIENT**
VIJF890 publishers
**URL**
www.fluff-sb.com
**COUNTRY**
The Netherlands

VARIOUS

**TITLE**
Adelle
**COMPANY**
TypeTogether
**CLIENT**
TypeTogether
**DESIGNERS**
Veronika Burian
José Scaglione
**COUNTRY**
Czech Republic

It's a multifunctional typeface, meant for text setting at small sizes as well as for titles. It has a personality that doesn't affect legibility. The family has a wide range of weights, making it useful in editorial applications.

# International

School tests for *7 and 11 years old* are constantly getting lower

# Modern time

Conference will be held in *Kopenhagen* in 2009

# Adelle ③

## *financial reviewers*

# Newsreel

Chic without the suffering: **FASHION DISPLAYS** its ethical face at

# "Responsibility"

## *Foreign policy makers*

TITLE
Premiéra
COMPANY
Typejockeys
DESIGNER
Thomas Gabriel
COUNTRY
Austria

# Premiéra

Book

abcdefghijklmnopqrstuvwxyz
ABCDEFGHIJKLMNOPQRSTUVWXYZ
123456789 123456789 (.,;:?!@&-®€$£♥)

*abcdefghijklmnopqrstuvwxyz*
*ABCDEFGHIJKLMNOPQRSTUVWXYZ*
*123456789 123456789 (.,;:?!@&-®€$£♥)*

Italic

Bold

**abcdefghijklmnopqrstuvwxyz**
**ABCDEFGHIJKLMNOPQRSTUVWXYZ**
**123456789 123456789 (.,;:?!@&-®€$£♥)**

# Rashōmon

## Amélie

## *Parfume*

### *Everything is illuminated*

### LES MISÉRABLES

Pendant une ou deux minutes elle res à regarder **LA MAISON** en se demaind ce qu'elle[1] allait *faire, lorsque,* soudain, valet de PIED EN LIVRÉE **sortit du boi** en courant (*elle se dit que c'était un valet pied parce qu'il était en livrée : mais à en ju*

**Lidt efter hørte hun nogle små fødder trippe i nærheden, og hun skyndte sig at tørre sine øjne for at se, hvem det var, der kom. Det var den hvide kanin, som vendte tilbage! Den var meget fin i tøjet og havde et par hvide handsker i den ene hånd og en stor vifte i den**

Casi sin saber lo que hacía, cogió del suelo una ramita seca y la levantó hacia el perrito, y el perrito dio un salto con las cuatro patas en el aire, soltó un ladrido de satisfacción y se abalanzó sobre el palo en gesto de ataque. Entonces Alicia se escabulló rápidamente tras un gran cardo, para no ser arrollada, y, en cuanto apareció por el otro lado, el cachorro volvió

Endlich nahm die Raupe die Huhka aus dem Munde und redete sie mit schmachtender, langsamer Stimme an. »Wer bist du?« fragte die Raupe. Das war kein sehr ermutigender Anfang einer Unterhaltung. Alice antwortete, etwas befangen: »Ich – ich weiß nicht recht, diesen Augenblick – vielmehr ich weiß, wer ich heut früh war, als ich aufstand; aber ich glaube, ich muß seitdem ein paar Mal verwechselt worden sein.« »Was meinst du damit?« sagte die Raupe strenge. »Erkläre dich deutlicher!« »Ich kann mich nicht deutlicher erklären, fürchte ich, Raupe,« sagte Alice, »weil ich es nicht weiß, sehen Sie wohl?« »Ich sehe nicht wohl,« sagte die Raupe. »Ich kann es wirklich nicht besser ausdrücken,« erwiederte Alice sehr höflich.

**ALICE WAS BEGINNING TO GET TIRED** of sitting by her sister on the bank, and of having nothing to do: once or twice she had peeped into the book her sister was reading, but it had no pictures or conversations in it, 'and what is the use

*Il pesce valletto cavò di sotto il braccio un letterone grande quasi quanto lui, e lo presentò all'altro, dicendo solennemente: «Per la Duchessa. Un invito della Regina per giocare una partita di croquet.» Il ranocchio valletto rispose nello stesso tono di voce, ma cambiando l'ordine delle parole: «Dalla Regina. Un invito per la Duches-*

There was nothing so very remarkable in that; nor did Alice think it so very much out of the way to hear the Rabbit say to itself, **'OH DEAR! OH DEAR! I SHALL BE LATE!'** (when she thought it over afterwards, it occurred to her that she ought to have wondered at this, but at the time it all seemed quite natural); but when the Rabbit actually took a watch out of

Pendant une ou deux minutes elle resta à regarder la maison en se demandant ce qu'elle allait faire, lorsque, soudain, un valet de PIED EN LIVRÉE sortit du bois en courant (*elle se dit que c'était un valet de pied parce qu'il était en livrée : mais à en juger seulement d'après son visage, elle l'aurait plutôt pris pour un poisson*), et frappa très fort à la porte de ses doigts repliés. Celle-ci fut ouverte par un autre valet de pied en livrée, au visage tout rond, aux gros yeux saillants comme ceux d'une grenouille ; Alice remarqua que les deux laquais avaient le crâne recouvert d'une chevelure poudrée et toute en boucles. Elle se sentait très curieuse de savoir de quoi il s'agissait, et elle se glissa un peu hors du bois pour écouter.

**TITLE**
Encore Sans Pro
**COMPANY**
Parachute
**CLIENT**
Parachute
**DESIGNER**
Panos Vassiliou
**COUNTRY**
Greece

ΕΛΛΗΝΟΛΑΤΙΝΙΚΟ ΜΕΙΓΜΑ ΜΕ ΠΡΟΣΦΑΤΕΣ ΚΥΡΙΛΛΙΚΕΣ ΠΡΟΣΜΕΙΞΕΙΣ

# τεχνολογική ανάπτυξη

*η αισιοδοξία είναι μια στρατηγική για ένα καλύτερο αύριο*

# ΡΕΖΕΡΒΑ

ΤΟ ΙΣΧΥΡΟΤΕΡΟ ΔΗΜΙΟΥΡΓΙΚΟ ΔΥΝΑΜΩΤΙΚΟ ΣΟΥ

## *εταιρική ταυτότητα*

Η τηλεόραση παρουσίασε ορισμένα προϊόντα και υπηρεσίες

**ΖΩΝΤΑΝΕΣ ΕΙΚΟΝΕΣ ΚΑΙ ΠΛΟΥΣΙΑ ΧΡΩΜΑΤΑ**

## *ταξιδιώτης*

**η αισθητική είναι η πολιτική του μέλλοντος**

ΜΕΣΟΓΕΙΑΚΗ ΚΟΥΖΙΝΑ

# κινηματογράφος

*ξενοδοχεία υψηλών προδιαγραφών με θέα το απέραντο γαλάζιο*

Ασχέτως αν τα έθνη παραμείνουν περιορισμένα από εδαφική άποψη ή γίνουν πιο διασκορπισμένα, η ηλεκτρονική γειτνίαση θα ενισχύσει τους πολιτιστικούς δεσμούς ανάμεσά τους. Στις λίγες δεκαετίες που η τηλεόραση διασκορπίστηκε παντού, διέδωσε ορισμένους πολιτιστικούς κανόνες, ακόμα και σε έθνη όπου τα ηλεκτρονικά μέσα ενημέρωσης απαγορεύονταν κατηγορηματικά. Η κατάρρευση της πρώην Σοβιετικής Ένωσης μπορεί να επηρεάστηκε από αυτό τον παράγοντα περισσότερο απ' όσο νομίζουμε. Η τηλεόραση παρουσίασε ορισμένα προϊόντα και υπηρεσίες σε όλο τον κόσμο, δίνοντας τη δυνατότητα στους ανθρώπους να τα θεωρούν κοινά, αν όχι να

# BRONZE
ORIGINAL TYPEFACE

**TITLE**
Archiv
**COMPANY**
Atalier Bubentraum
**COUNTRY**
Switzerland

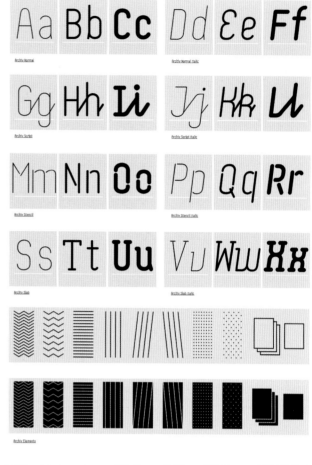

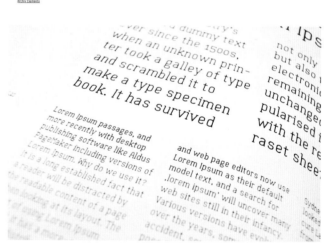

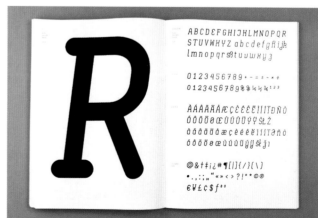

TITLE
DSIGNES typeface
COMPANY
Andreu Balius
CLIENT
SIGNES
COUNTRY
Spain

ENTRADA ↗ EINGANG ↘ WPIS → ENTRY ↑ BELÉPÉS ↘ VSTUPU → ULAZ
OPPFØRING → KANNE → VNOS ↗ ENTRATA ↓ BINNENKOMST ↗ ENTRÉE

# NORTE·SUR·ESTE·OESTE

# DSIGNES

TIPOGRAFÍA DISEÑADA PARA LA EMPRESA **SIGNES** POR → ANDREU BALIUS 2008-2009 (A typeface specially designed for signal system purposes)

ABCÇDEFGHIJKLMNÑOPQ
RSTUVWXYZ0123456789
abcçdefghijklmnñopqrstuv
wxyz*(¿"@"?){$£¥€¢}©®™
ĐŽŠŁŸÆŒØÅÕßfifl†‡«»#§[¶]
& etc... ← → ↓ ↑          Dsignes Light

ABCÇDEFGHIJKLMNÑOPQ
RSTUVWXYZ0123456789
abcçdefghijklmnñopqrstuv
wxyz*(¿"@"?){$£¥€¢}©®™
ĐŽŠŁŸÆŒØÅÕßfifl†‡«»#§[¶]
& etc... ← → ↓ ↑        Dsignes Regular

**ABCÇDEFGHIJKLMNÑOPQ
RSTUVWXYZ0123456789
abcçdefghijklmnñopqrstuv
wxyz*(¿"@"?){$£¥€¢}©®™
ĐŽŠŁŸÆŒØÅÕßfifl†‡«»#§[¶]
& etc... ← → ↓ ↑          Dsignes Bold**

# L'HOSPITALET DE LLOBREGAT

# BARCELONA

**Siempre llegarás a alguna parte, si caminas lo bastante –dijo el gato a Alicia**

# Tots els camins porten a Roma

# HIGHWAY TO HELL

**Las señales de humo son aquellas que se utilizan para la comunicación entre áreas vastas y despobladas**

# La Estrella Polar señala el norte

# WAY OUT

**TITLE**
Karmina Sans
**COMPANY**
TypeTogether
**COUNTRY**
Czech Republic

**TITLE**
Genetika typeface system
**COMPANY**
Gobranding.eu
**COUNTRY**
Poland

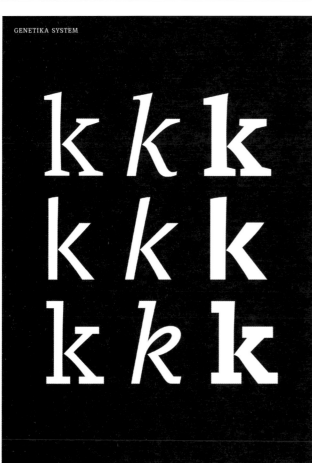

**TITLE**
Al Ittihad custom typeface
**COMPANY**
Monotype Imaging
**CLIENT**
Al Ittihad
**COUNTRY**
United Kingdom

ء ا ا ىب ب ت تت ت ثث ث تث ث جج ج ححح ح خخ خ خخخ خ

د د ذ ر ز سسس س شش ش ششش ش صص ص ضض

ض ض ططط ط ظظظ ظ ععع ع غغغ غ ففف ف ققق ق

ككك ك للل ل ممم م ننن ن هه هه ة ة و و يي يي ي

آ آ أ أ إ إ لا لا لآ لآ لأ لأ لإ لإ ى ى ؤ ؤ ئئئ 0123456789

Arabic custom typeface for a national newspaper

الإمارات

الاقتصادي أسواق الإمارات

عربي ودولي

الثقافي أحوال    الثقافي سيرة

الرياضي

الثقافي زمن البدايات    الثقافي نقد

وجهات نظر

Custom headline type family for a newspaper

TITLE
Al Ittihad custom
headline type family
COMPANY
Monotype Imaging
CLIENT
Al Ittihad
COUNTRY
United Kingdom

بلاغ رسمي

«اقتصادية أبوظبي» و «التجارة البريطانية» تؤكدان أهمية التعاون الاستثماري

اتفاقية لتطوير الفرص التكنولوجية بين الإمارات وبريطانيا

حلف شمال الاطلسي تجتمع 26 أكتوبر الجاري

الانفتاح الدبلوماسي

154 مليون درهم قيمة مساعدات
«الهلال الأحمر» للسودان منذ 1970

ضغوط هائلة

الاحتفال بختام مشروع
إزالة الألغام في لبنان

العلاقات المصرية خصام سياسي وحميمية ثقافية

مد وجزر عمره خمسة قرون

ء ا ا بيب ب تتت ت
ثث ث ججج ج ححح ح
خخخ خ ـد دد ـذ ذ ـر رز
سسس س ششش ش
صصص ص ضضض ض
طط ط ظظظ ظ ععع
ع غغغ غ ففف ف ققق
ق ككك ك للل ل ممم م
ننن ن ههه ه ة ة و و
ييي ي آ آ أ أ إ إ لا لا لآ
لآ لأ لأ لإ لإ ى ـؤ ؤ
نئ ى ([0123456789])
%...،.ٌ:؛؟!ٍ*()ٍ»«
ً ٌٍ ۥ ۥ / ‚‚"""

ء ا ا بيب ب تتت ت
ثث ث ججج ج ححح ح
خخخ خ ـد دد ـذ ذ ـر رز
سسس س ششش ش
صصص ص ضضض ض
طط ط ظظظ ظ ععع
ع غغغ غ ففف ف ققق
ق ككك ك للل ل ممم م
ننن ن ههه ه ة ة و و
ييي ي آ آ أ أ إ إ لا لا لآ
لآ لأ لأ لإ لإ ى ـؤ ؤ
نئ ى ([0123456789])
%...،.ٌ:؛؟!ٍ*()ٍ»«
ً ٌٍ ۥ ۥ / ‚‚"""

Increased word-unit definition

| Within a word | End or beginning |
|---|---|
| لا د ع | لا د ع |

بالرغم من بعض
الانعكاسات السلبية
التي خلفتها الأزمة
علينا إلا أنها أثبتت
متانة اقتصادنا

**TITLE**
Fenafresh
**COMPANY**
designersunited.gr
**CLIENT**
Fenafresh
**COUNTRY**
Greece

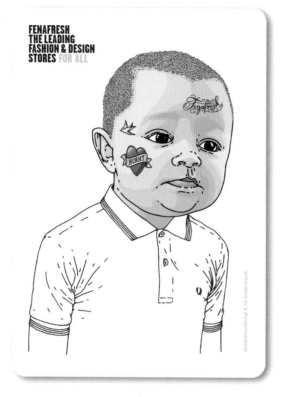

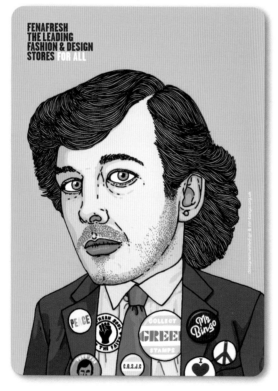

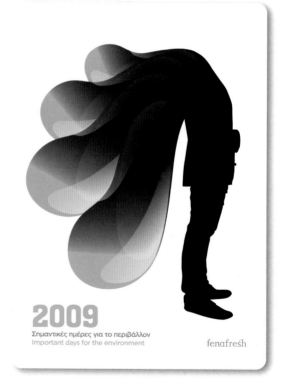

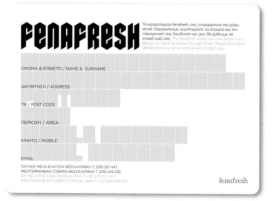

# GOLD
## CALENDAR

**TITLE**
Create A Beautiful Image
**COMPANY**
Ando bv
**CLIENT**
Ando bv
**DESIGNER**
Yu Zhao
**ART DIRECTOR**
Edwin Van Praet
**CREATIVE DIRECTOR**
Total Identity
**COPYWRITER**
Erik Mastebroek
**PRINTERS**
Ando Bv
Fokko Tamminga
**COUNTRY**
The Netherlands

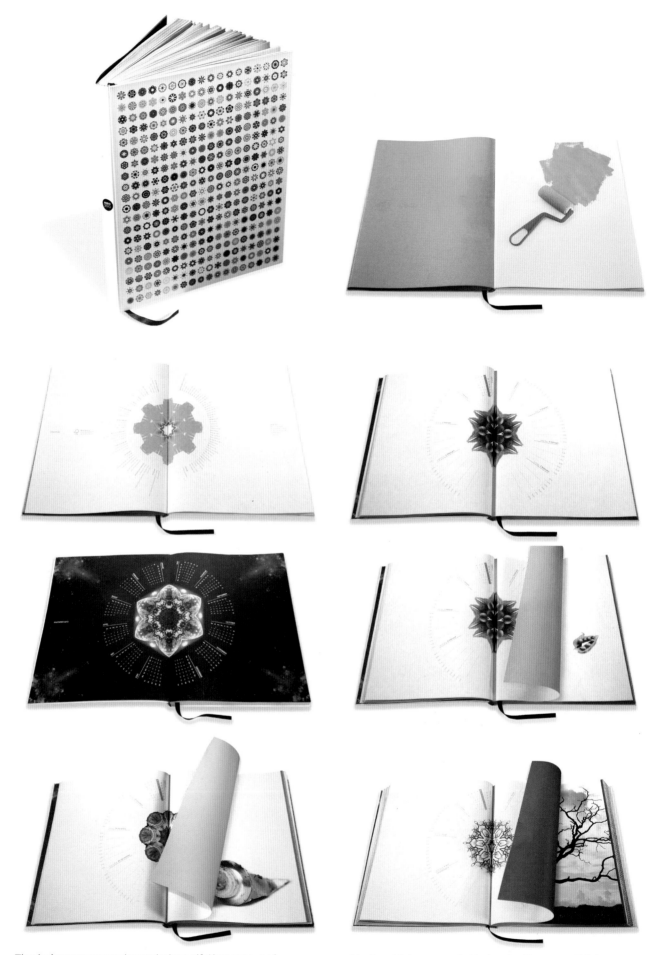

The designers managed to make beautiful images out of very common objects, which are revealed by tearing the pages: this becomes an invitation to the receiver to make the best of their time, and to see beauty in the tiniest things. The use of colour nicely counterbalances the images. This calendar can be effectively used as a diary, thanks to the wide amount of white space, and gives the user the sense of discovery: every week a new object can be found.

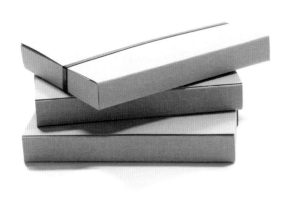

**TITLE**
Spinhex & Industry 2010
**COMPANY**
Lava
**CLIENT**
Spinhex & Industry
**DESIGNER**
Reza Abedini
**ART DIRECTOR**
Anne Miltenburg
**COUNTRY**
The Netherlands

The tactile aspect of this calendar is important: humble materials become interesting through printing and die-cuts. The monthly envelopes reveal 12 little gifts, objects made out of paper and cardboard. Graphics and typography show an interesting way to connect eastern and western visual cultures.

**TITLE**
Verplant 2010
**COMPANY**
JUNO
**CLIENT**
Peyer Graphic GmbH
**DESIGNERS**
Wolfgang Greter
Barbara Schwitzke
Christoph Lohse
**ART DIRECTOR**
Wolfgang Greter
**CREATIVE DIRECTORS**
Wolfgang Greter
Björn Lux
**EDITOR**
Juno
**COUNTRY**
Germany

**TITLE**
Typodarium 2010
**COMPANY**
MAGMA
Brand Design GmbH & Co. KG
**CLIENT**
Verlag Hermann Schmidt Mainz
**ART DIRECTORS**
Boris Kahl
Daniela Sattler
**CREATIVE DIRECTORS**
Lars Harmsen
Raban Ruddigkeit
**EDITORS**
Uli Weiss
Tanja Rastätter
Julia Kahl
**COUNTRY**
Germany

**TITLE**
Calendar-Mousepad
**COMPANY**
DarkDesignGroup
**CLIENT**
DarkDesignGroup
**URL**
darkdesign.ru
**COUNTRY**
Russia

**TITLE**
2010 calendar
**COMPANY**
jurczyk design
**CLIENT**
Antalis Poland
**COUNTRY**
Poland

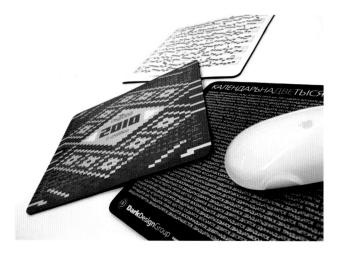
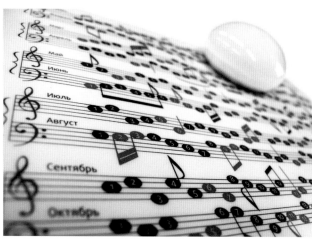

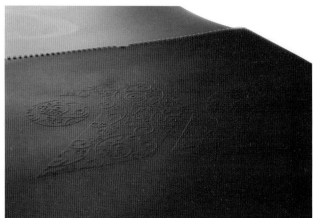

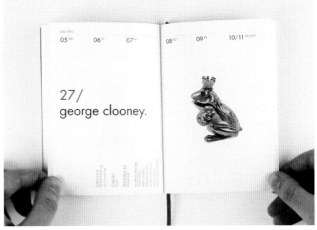

**FINALIST**
CALENDAR

**TITLE**
Agenda 2010 -
A new sort of calendar
**COMPANY**
Markwald und Neusitzer
Kommunikationsdesign GbR
**CLIENT**
Markwald & Neusizuer
Kommunikationsdesign
**COUNTRY**
Germany

**TITLE**
Starogard Herbal Diary
**COMPANY**
Starogard Gdański Municipality
**CLIENT**
Starogard Gdański Municipality
**COUNTRY**
Poland

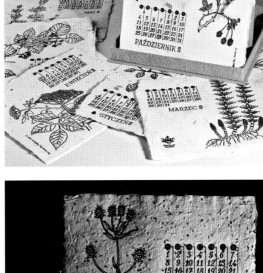

**TITLE**
Design Walk 2009
**COMPANY**
the design shop
**CLIENT**
Design Walk
**ART DIRECTORS**
Dionysis Livanis
**COUNTRY**
Greece

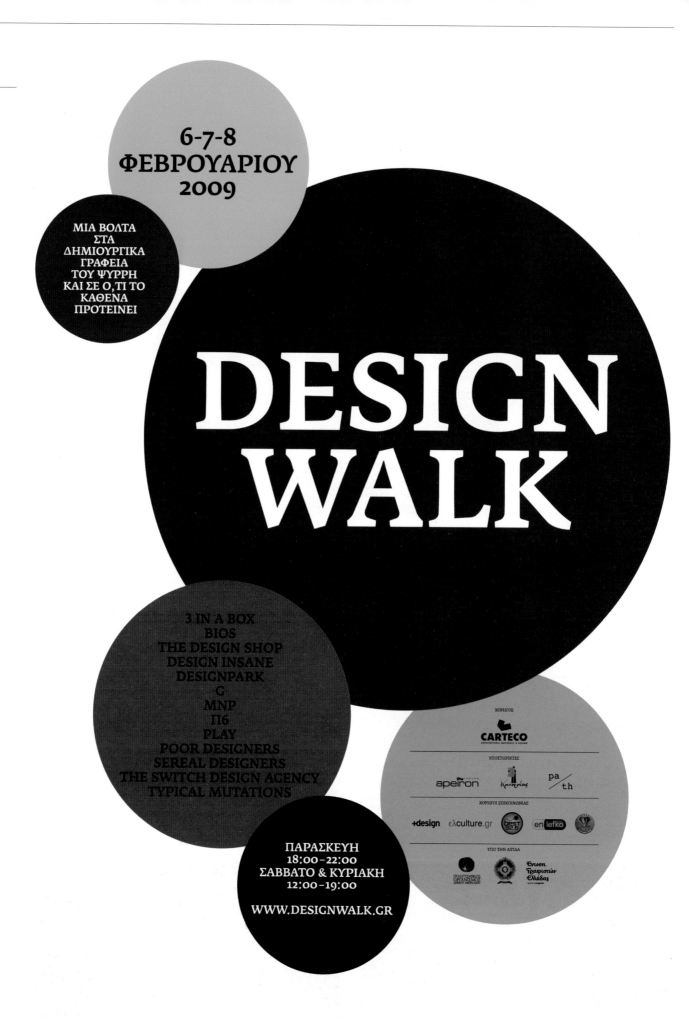

The Design Walks posters go beyond the usual poster format to become also a kind of navigation system to the studios involved in the event. Being made of five elements to be freely assembled, it integrates very well in the urban landscape: once it's posted, it seems like it really belongs there.

**TITLE**
Lausanne Underground
Film & Music Festival
**COMPANY**
Notter + Vigne
**CLIENT**
Lausanne Underground
Film & Music Festival
**DESIGNER**
Notter + Vigne
**COUNTRY**
Switzerland

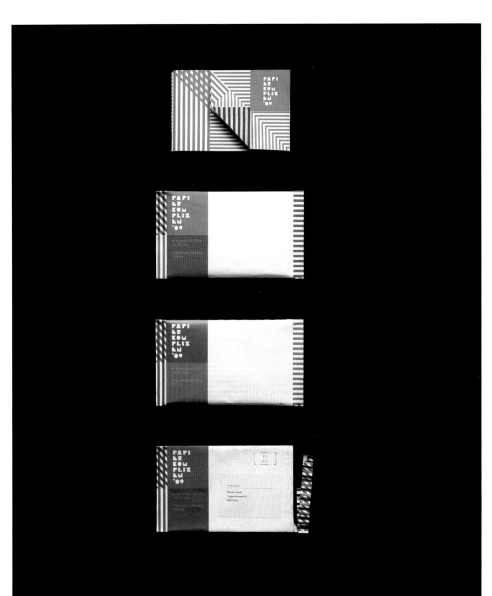

**TITLE**
Papierkomplizen '09
**COMPANY**
Viola Zimmermann
**CLIENT**
Buchbinderei Burkhardt AG
Fischer Papier AG
Sonderegger AG
**COUNTRY**
Switzerland

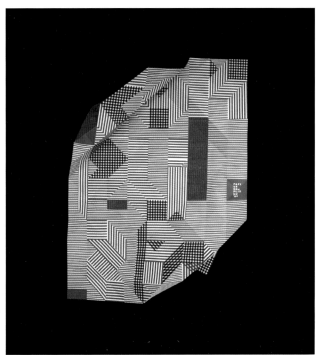

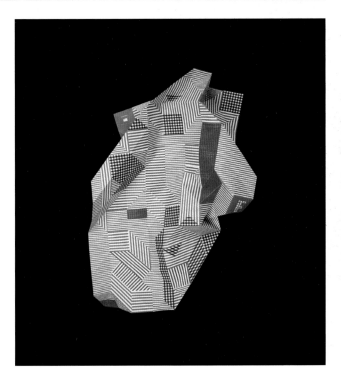

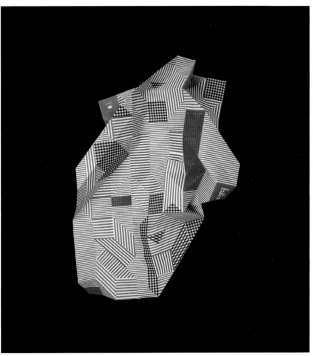

**TITLE**
PULLY fireworks
**COMPANY**
enzed
**CLIENT**
Ville de Pully
**COUNTRY**
Switzerland

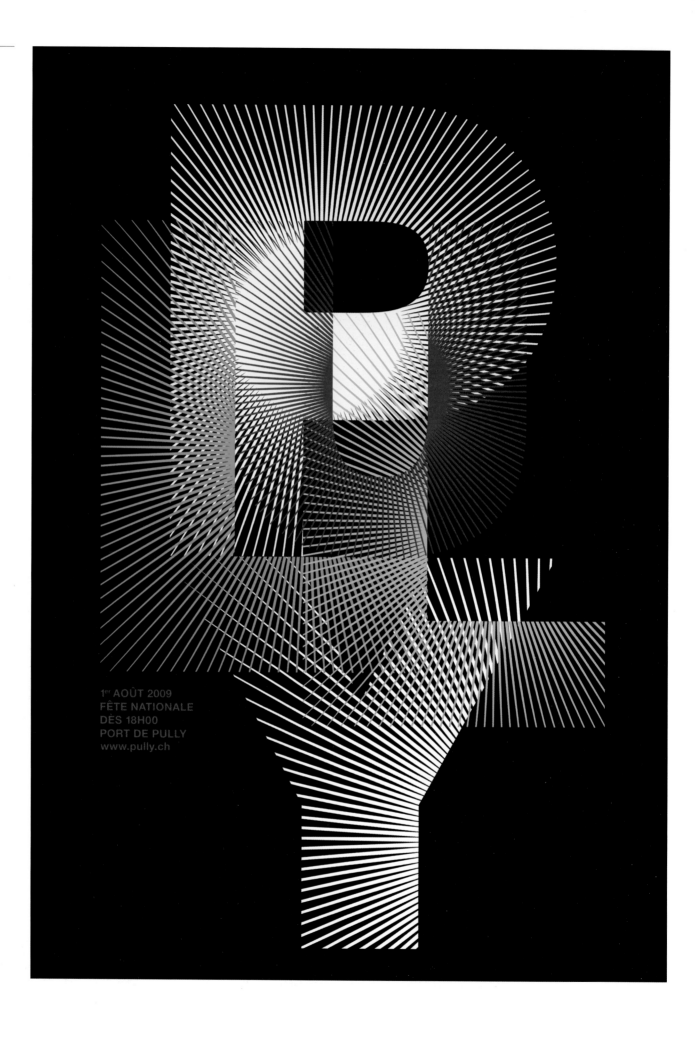

1er AOÛT 2009
FÊTE NATIONALE
DÈS 18H00
PORT DE PULLY
www.pully.ch

**TITLE**
Exhibition poster
"Democratic Design - Ikea"
**COMPANY**
Die Neue Sammlung
The International Design
Museum Munich
**CLIENT**
Die Neue Sammlung
The International Design
Museum Munich
**COUNTRY**
Germany

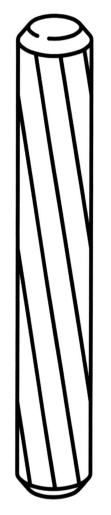

# Democratic Design
# I K E A
# 3.4.09 – 12.7.09

101375

16x

Die Neue Sammlung
The International Design Museum Munich
Barer Straße 40
Pinakothek der Moderne
München
www.die-neue-sammlung.de
In Kooperation mit IKEA

**TITLE**
The Invisible Frame -
Film Poster
**COMPANY**
Moniteurs GmbH
**CLIENT**
Filmgalerie 451
**COUNTRY**
Germany

**TITLE**
Delta awards 09
**COMPANY**
David Torrents
**CLIENT**
ADIFAD
**COUNTRY**
Spain

**TITLE**
Ander Art
**COMPANY**
Büro Alba
**CLIENT**
Landeshauptstadt
München Kulturreferat
**COUNTRY**
Germany

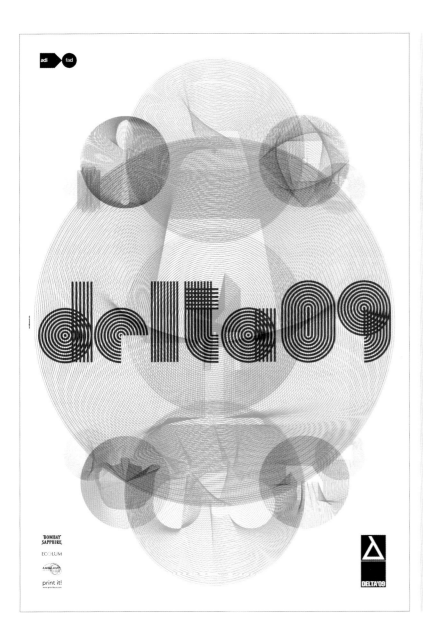

# GOLD
POSTER SERIES

**TITLE**
Omofobia
**COMPANY**
Studio FM Milano
**CLIENT**
Milano Contro l'Omofobia
**DESIGNER**
Cristiano Bottino
**ART DIRECTOR**
Studio Fm Milano
**CREATIVE DIRECTOR**
Cristiano Bottino
**COUNTRY**
Italy

As the entry level of this category was high, the jury was looking for something that went beyond pure design excellence and discussed an important contemporary issue. This poster series comes at a time when Italy has witnessed many episodes of intolerance against gay people. The portraits of leaders from past and contemporary totalitarian regimes, known for their persecution of homosexuals, are rendered typographically using the letters that form the word "omofobia": although this typographical treatment is not completely new, we feel it manages to convey the existence of homophobia in a subtle way.

# {FASCISMO}

Gay e lesbiche vennero perseguitati in base al Testo Unico delle Leggi di Pubblica Sicurezza (Regio Decreto n.773 del 18-6-1931), che dava alla polizia il potere decisionale di eliminare dalla convivenza sociale (senza necessità di processi) qualunque individuo tenesse un atteggiamento ritenuto "scandaloso".
Oltre al pestaggi, allo stigma sociale e all'olio di ricino, ad un individuo omosessuale potevano toccare le sorte la diffida, l'ammonizione e il confino (oristineamente noto l'isolotto di San Domino, nelle Tremiti).

A seguito della promulgazione delle Leggi per la difesa della razza, l'Italia fascista tendi ad allinearsi alla Germania nazista anche nelle motivazioni ideologiche della persecuzione omosessuale. Gli omosessuali vennero classificati come confinati politici, anziché come confinati comuni.
Nessun riconoscimento è stato ad oggi concesso alle vittime omosessuali della persecuzione fascista. A nessuno dei confinati politici gay è stata concessa la relativa pensione rioarcitoria. Nessuna riabilitazione è stata ammessa per le persone che hanno sofferto la persecuzione fascista. Nonostante i ripetuti richiami da parte del Parlamento Europeo, nessun Governo della Repubblica Italiana è stato ad oggi in grado di approvare alcuna legge che punisca la discriminazione e gli atti di violenza base sull'orientamento sessuale (legge contro l'omofobia).

# {CUBA}

"Una **deviazione** di questa natura si scontra con il concetto che abbiamo di ciò che un militante comunista deve essere."

*Fidel Castro*

Nel 1959 **Fidel Castro** salì al potere a Cuba. Già due anni dopo i primi omosessuali, considerati dei controrivoluzionari e dei malati, iniziarono ad essere rinchiusi nelle Unità Militari di Aiuto alla Produzione (UMAP), i campi di lavoro forzati creati da Ernesto Guevara, detto il Che. Per essere imprigionati non occorrevano processi, bastava il sospetto di un vicino. Il consolidamento del regime non attenuò più di tanto le discriminazioni contro gli omosessuali ai quali era impedita un'istruzione universitaria, erano vietati i lavori a contatto diretto con il pubblico ed era negata la tessera del partito che con conseguenti difficoltà a trovare un lavoro a una casa. Tutt'oggi, il codice penale, all'articolo 303, condanna chi offende il pudore e il buon costume con esibizioni, atti e pubblicazioni oscene mettendo di fatto fuori legge la pubblica manifestazione dell'omosessualità.

# {NAZISMO}

L'omosessualità era punita in Germania sin dalla nascita dello stato nazionale, nel 1871, secondo la lettera del paragrafo 175 del codice penale del Secondo Reich che recitava: "Gli atti vosceri contro natura, commessi tra persone di sesso maschile e da uomini con bestie, sono puniti dal carcere; si può anche pronunciare la perdita dei diritti civili onorifici". Nonostante questo, in quegli anni cominciò a svilupparsi il primo movimento al mondo per i diritti degli omosessuali e Berlino divenne la città più gay-friendly del mondo giungendo ad avere, nel 1930, 80 locali omosessuali, 20 riviste e 2 case editrici specializzate. Dopo l'ascesa al potere di Hitler nel gennaio 1933, il nazismo, il paragrafo 175, inasprì la normativa anti-omosessuale con il paragrafo 175/A che arrivava a sanzionare persino le fantasie omosessuali. Già nel luglio 1934 il giurista Rudolf Klare aveva esposto la posizione ufficiale del partito nazionalsocialista nei riguardi dell'omosessualità che vedeva più volte ripresa da Himmler; la purezza della razza doveva essere salvaguardata attraverso l'eliminazione dei degenerati. Dopo la caduta del regime il paragrafo 175 venne abolito dalla DDR nel 1948, ma solo nel 1969 dalla Germania occidentale. Solo nel settembre 2001 è stato annunciato un risarcimento agli omosessuali vittime del nazismo e nel maggio 2002 il Parlamento tedesco ha chiesto ufficialmente scusa.

Tra il 1933 e il 1945 le persone processate per violazione del paragrafo 175 furo **60.000**, di questi circa **10.000** vennero internati nei campi di concentramento.
Gli altri furono condannati a pene detentive.
I morti accertati tra il 1933 e il 1945 furono circa **7000**.

# {CINA}

Il regime comunista, instaurato in Cina nel 1949, considerava l'omosessualità una forma di malattia mentale e un problema di ordine pubblico.
Sia l'omosessualità maschile, sia quella femminile erano pertanto punite in base all'articolo del codice penale che sanzionava il teppismo.
Il momento di maggior persecuzione fu la Rivoluzione culturale (1966-69), in quel periodo molti gay furono puniti con lunghi periodi di internamento nei lager" (i campi di lavoro cinesi) e non mancò qualche esecuzione. La tolleranza sociale dell'omosessualità era lievemente fitto con la politica definita di "Riforma ed apertura" del 1979. Il comunismo mutò ed allentare la sua forte funzione di controllo su queste tipo di comportamento, anche se la pratica dell'omosessualità continuò ad essere ritenuta diffamante e veniva identificata come uno stile di vita dissoluto tipico del regimi capitalistici.
Un cambiamento silenzioso si registrò nel 1997, quando l'omosessualità venne decriminalizzata e nel 2001 quando venne rimossa dalla lista delle malattie mentali. Da allora la Cina adotta sull'omosessualità la regola dei 3 no: no approvazione, no disapprovazione e no promozione.

# {URSS}

Con la Rivoluzione d'Ottobre del 1917 vennero abrogate tutte le leggi zariste, anche quelle contro l'omosessualità; il codice penale zarista del 1832 punivaa la mutilazione con l'esilio in Siberia fino a 5 anni. Il "Codice delle Pene" del 1903, com'l'art. 996, aumentava il confino a 12 anni e lo accompagnava ai lavori forzati. Fu tradita a ristabilire la condanna dell'omosessualità nel 1934 per motivi di lotta interna mascherati da voceperazione di polizia morale con l'art. 154a l'omosessualità divenuva un reato politico e un'attività controrivoluzionaria, "intollerabile nella società socialista, grave fenomeno di degenerazione morale". Nel 1961 Khrushov, il promotore della destalinizzazione, varò una riforma del codice penale che, rettaola, mantenenva, all'art. 121, la condanna dell'omosessualità rimossa dall'ordinamento giuridico russo solo nel 1993.

In totale sono stati condannati alla deportazione nei *Gulag*° circa **50.000** omosessuali.

# {IRAN}

"Non ci sono gay in Iran, le donne sono trattate meglio degli uomini."

*Mahmud Ahmadinejad*

Dalla rivoluzione islamica del 1979, il governo iraniano ha mandato a morte più di 4000 persone arrestate ai rapporti omosessuali secondo l'articolo 111 del codice penale islamico che sanziona il crimine di liwat. Come si legge nei documenti della Federazione internazionale dei rifugiati iraniani si può essere giustiziati per: impiccagione, lapidazione, "trancamento per mezzo di una spada", "precipitazione dal picco più alto".

L'organizzazione Human Rights Watch documenta che il regime iraniano non persegulita soltanto gli atti sessuali tra persone dello stesso sesso, ma ogni altra forma di atto erosexnico non penetrativo, o labby, punibile con cento frustate per ciascuno dei partner e con la condanna a morte per i soggetti recidivi in seguito alla quarta condanna. Ancora, due persone di sesso maschile che giacciono nude "nello stesso luogo senza necessità" sono punite con 99 frustate. Spesso la condanna di omosessualità, sia contro uomini che contro donne, è utilizzata come strumento di persecuzione politica.

**TITLE**
Historias
**COMPANY**
virgen extra
**CLIENT**
David Puente
**DESIGNER**
Ismael Medina
**CREATIVE DIRECTORS**
Ismael Medina
Sebas Cangiano
**COPYWRITER**
Sebas Cangiano
**COUNTRY**
Spain

Sintió sus labios, casi empalagosos y siempre inolvidables, por última vez hace 273 años. Aquella mujer que lo poseía por completo desapareció para siempre, sin decir adiós, sin mentir y sin mirar hacia atrás. Y desde entonces, aquella copa sólo hace una cosa: preguntarse por qué.

*Todo tiene una historia que contar.*
DAVID PUENTE. ANTIGÜEDADES.

Nadie sabía cuánto deseaba dejar de ser inmortal. Tener la esperanza de que habría un final. Y ese día doblar sus extremidades y descansar. Nadie sabía cuánto deseaba dejar de ser esa soberbia silla del siglo XV.

*Todo tiene una historia que contar.*
DAVID PUENTE. ANTIGÜEDADES.

Escribas. Príncipes. Bufones. Verdugos. Y asesinos. Alquimistas. Científicos. Cowboys. Maquinistas. Ilusionistas. Doctores. Ingenieros aeronáuticos. Hippies. Un astronauta. Vendedores de humo. Abogados especialistas en derecho aduanero. Dos diputados provinciales. Y una secretaria que estaba enamorada de su compañera de trabajo. Y todos ellos transformados en esas imágenes, tan reales y, al mismo tiempo, ficticias, que sólo un espejo vetusto y experimentado es capaz de regalar.

*Todo tiene una historia que contar.*
DAVID PUENTE. ANTIGÜEDADES.

Era un reloj. Y en un principio mi función consistía en indicar la hora. Definir inequívocamente el presente, expresado en matemáticas horas y milimétricos segundos. Curiosamente, con el paso de los años hago todo lo contrario. Grito silenciosamente "soy parte del pasado". Y mis agujas descansan en paz. Elegantes y distinguidas. Como siempre lo fueron. Como siempre lo serán.

*Todo tiene una historia que contar.*
DAVID PUENTE. ANTIGÜEDADES.

TITLE
Retourtje Romeinen
COMPANY
SILO
CLIENT
Dutch Army Museum
COUNTRY
The Netherlands

**TITLE**
Boekenweek 2010
**COMPANY**
Designpolitie
**CLIENT**
CPNB
**COUNTRY**
The Netherlands

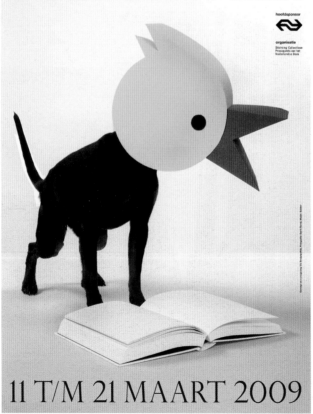

**TITLE**
GuitarraMadrid 2009
**COMPANY**
Iván Solbes SL
**CLIENT**
La Bikina
**COUNTRY**
Spain

# BRONZE
POSTER SERIES

**TITLE**
Projekt 100 - 2009
**COMPANY**
Bohdan Kofila Heblík
**CLIENT**
Asociace českých
filmových klubů
**COUNTRY**
Czech Republic

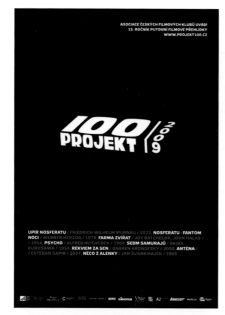

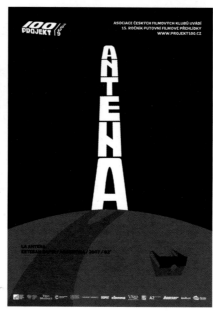

**TITLE**
Brecht Festival Augsburg 2010
**COMPANY**
KW Neun Grafikagentur
**CLIENT**
Kulturamt der Stadt Augsburg
**COUNTRY**
Germany

**TITLE**
De Balie Posterseries
**COMPANY**
Lava
**CLIENT**
De Balie
**COUNTRY**
The Netherlands

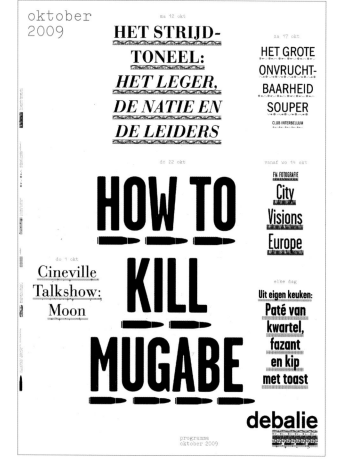

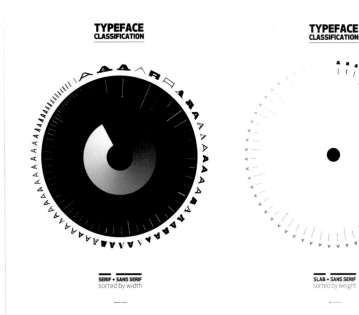

**FINALIST**
POSTER SERIES

**TITLE**
Typeface classification posters
**COMPANY**
This Is Tomorrow
**CLIENT**
This Is Tomorrow
**COUNTRY**
United Kingdom

**TITLE**
2009/2010 theatre posters
**COMPANY**
xhoch4 | design plus kultur
**CLIENT**
Ingolstadt Theatre
**COUNTRY**
Germany

**TITLE**
Building for the 2000-Watt
Society: The State of Affairs
**COMPANY**
Raffinrie AG
**CLIENT**
City of Zurich
**DESIGNERS**
Simon Fuhrimann
Helen Pombo
**CREATIVE DIRECTORS**
Christian Haas
Nenad Kovacic
**EDITORS**
Daniel Kurz
Karin Vasella-Kuhn
Anna Blattert
Tanja Reimer
Paul Knsel
**EXHIBITION CURATORS**
Karin Vasella-Kuhn
Daniel Kurz
**BUILT-UP**
**TECHNIQUE**
Holzer Kobler Architekturen
**COUNTRY**
Switzerland

This exhibition manages to have a striking impact with small means: it's an impressive structure which can be folded away, and the choice of materials is consistent with the main theme (sustainability in architecture). The information is displayed with different levels of detail according to the position in the installation: big headlines, pictures and small text are all part of a whole that remains consistent.

**TITLE**
Triennale Design Museum
**COMPANY**
Studio FM Milano
**CLIENT**
Triennale di Milano
**COUNTRY**
Italy

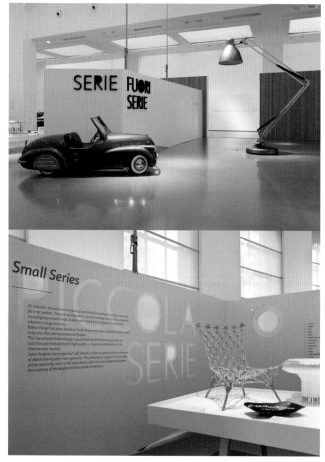

**TITLE**
OK
**COMPANY**
bauer konzept & gestaltung
gmbh
**CLIENT**
OK Offenes Kulturhaus
**DESIGNERS**
Erwin K. Bauer
Michael Herzog
Angie Rattay
**ARCHITECTURE**
Riepl Riepl Architecture
**COUNTRY**
Austria

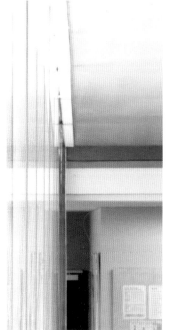

# SILVER
SIGNS & DISPLAYS

**TITLE**
Bikeway Belém / Cais do Sodré
**COMPANY**
P-06 atelier
ambientes e comunicação
lda
**CLIENT**
APL
administração do porto de lisboa
Lda
**DESIGNERS**
Giuseppe Greco
Miguel Matos
**ART DIRECTORS**
Nuno Gusmão
Estela Pinto
Pedro Anjos
**CREATIVE DIRECTORS**
Nuno Gusmão
João Gomes da Silva
**PHOTOGRAPHERS**
João Silveira Ramos
Giuseppe Greco
**FABRICATORS**
CME
ELECTROESTÚDIO
**COUNTRY**
Portugal

**TITLE**
Ecole des Petites-Fontaines
**COMPANY**
compactlab
**CLIENT**
Commune de Plan-les-Ouates
**DESIGNER**
Mauren Brodbeck
**ART DIRECTOR**
Oliver Rubli
**CREATIVE DIRECTORS**
Mauren Brodbeck
Oliver Rubli
**COUNTRY**
Switzerland

**TITLE**
Utrecht Uitfeest Leidsche Rijn
**COMPANY**
Autobahn
**CLIENT**
Beyond Leidsche Rijn
**COUNTRY**
The Netherlands

**TITLE**
44th Dimitria Festival
**COMPANY**
Beetroot Design Group
**CLIENT**
Municipality Of Thessaloniki/
Department Of Culture & Youth
**COUNTRY**
Greece

# FINALIST
SIGNS & DISPLAYS

**TITLE**
Westendgate Signage
**COMPANY**
BergmannStudios
**CLIENT**
Just / Burgeff Architetcts
**COUNTRY**
Germany

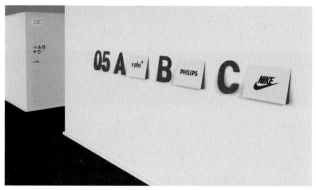

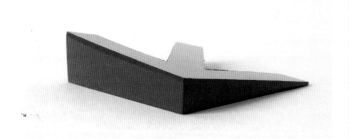

**TITLE**
Internal and External
Environmental Graphics
**COMPANY**
Holmes Wood
**CLIENT**
The Whitechapel Gallery
**COUNTRY**
United Kingdom

**TITLE**
Finding my European identity
**COMPANY**
motasdesign
**CLIENT**
Europeum Congress
& Event Centre
**COUNTRY**
Austria

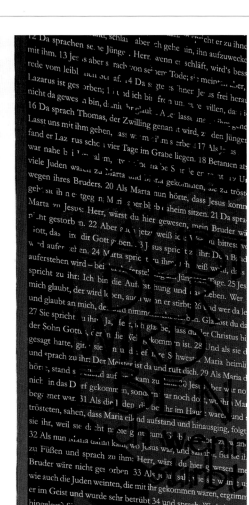

**FINALIST**
SIGNS & DISPLAYS

TITLE
Nassig - church windows
**COMPANY**
raumkontakt gmbh
**CLIENT**
parish of Nassig
**COUNTRY**
Germany

**TITLE**
Leitsystem für Demenz
Erkrankte
**DESIGNER**
Teresa Kettner
**EDITOR**
Teresa Kettner
**ILLUSTRATOR**
Teresa Kettner
**PHOTOGRAPHERS**
Patricia Plangger
Teresa Kettner
**COUNTRY**
Austria

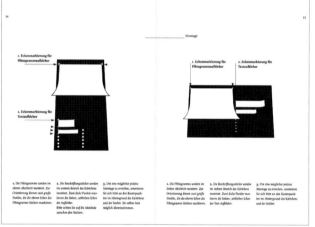

The project addresses a difficult problem head-on, providing the patient's relatives with a tool they can use to help to improve the quality of life. This modular system is easily adaptable to every person's specific needs.

### Informationsdichte

Die Anzahl und der Informationsgehalt
der Kärtchen können auf die verschie-
denen Stadien der Demenz angepasst
werden. Anfangs werden vielleicht nur
ein paar wenige Kärtchen benötigt, nur
um an den Platz der wichtigsten Alltags-
gegenstände zu erinnern.

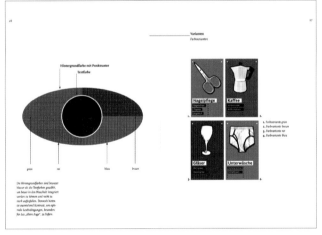

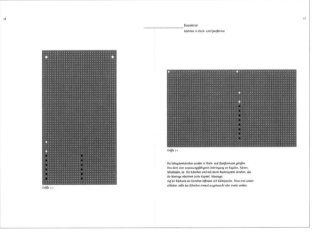

**TITLE**
13th Book Fair in Krakow
**DESIGNER**
DAGMARA BERSKA
**COUNTRY**
Poland

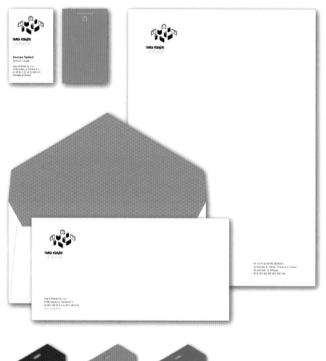

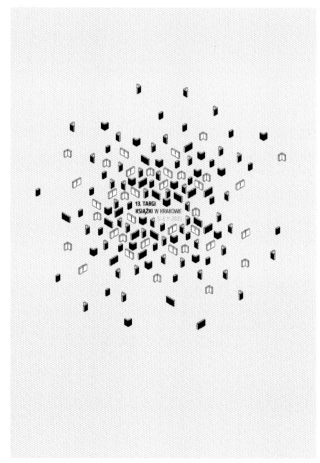

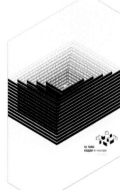

**TITLE**
Zweitgedanken
**DESIGNER**
Christian Jackmuth
**ILLUSTRATOR**
Christian Jackmuth
**PHOTOGRAPHER**
Christian Jackmuth
**COUNTRY**
Germany

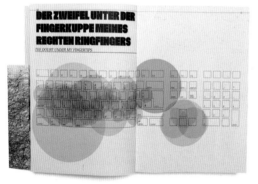

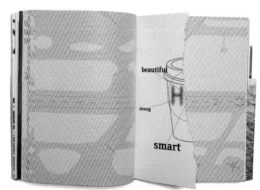

**BRONZE**
STUDENT PROJECTS

**TITLE**
drumatic
**DESIGNER**
René Andritsch
**CLIENT**
University
for the Creative Arts, UK
**COUNTRY**
Austria

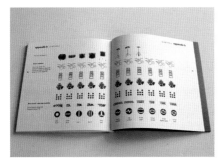

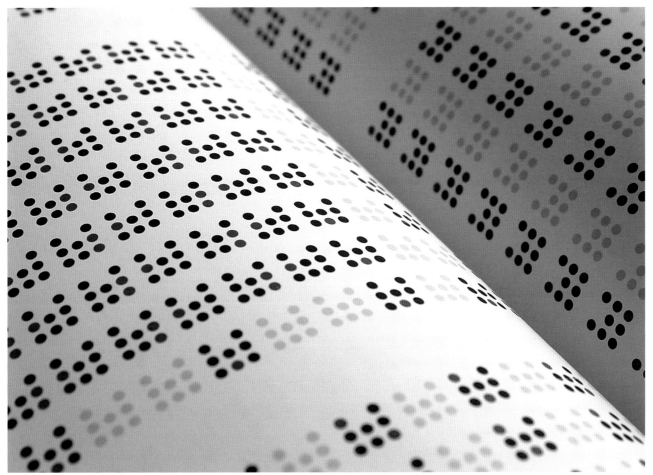

**TITLE**
dbc – death by chocolate
**DESIGNER**
Denise Franke
**CLIENT**
Folkwang University, Essen
**URL**
www.dfact.de/dbc
**COUNTRY**
Germany

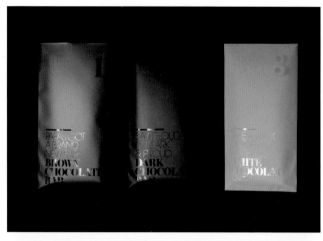

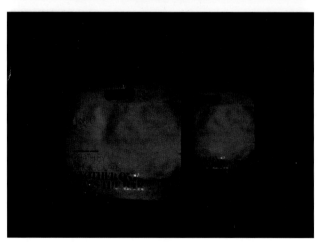
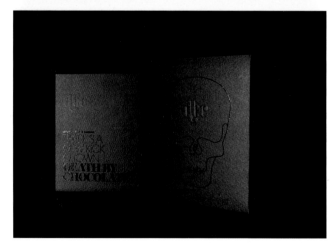

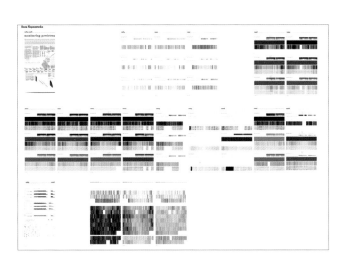

**TITLE**
Air Quality Monitoring
**DESIGNER**
Anna Kopaczewska
**CLIENT**
Intitute for Ecology of Industrial
Areas in Katowice (Poland)
**COUNTRY**
Poland

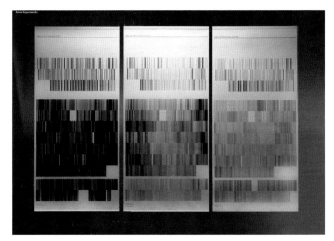

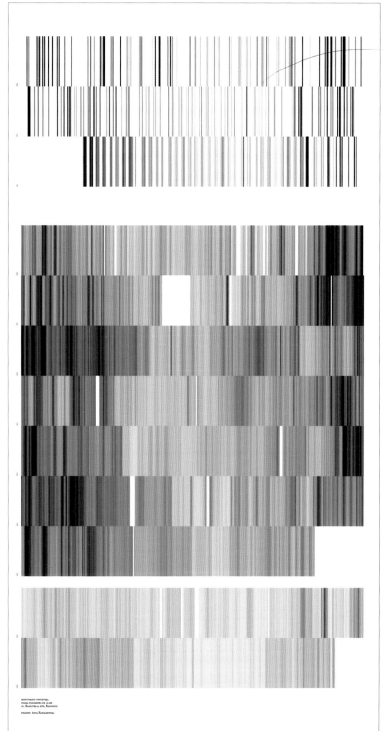

**TITLE**
Spamtastic
**DESIGNER**
Tina Mertlbauer
**COUNTRY**
Germany

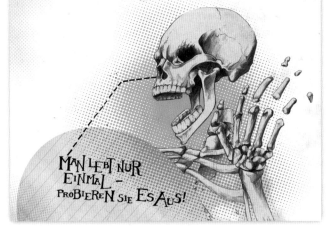

**TITLE**
Ucon - Deep Search
**COMPANY**
www.lvmonkiewitsch.de
**CLIENT**
Ucon Architecture Acrobatics
**URL**
www.ucon-acrobatics.com/
deepsearch
**COUNTRY**
Germany

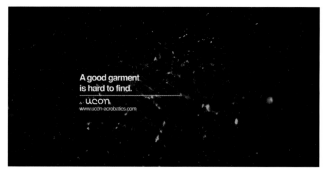

**TITLE**
Mooi Nederland 2009
**COMPANY**
SILO
**CLIENT**
TNTPost
**COUNTRY**
The Netherlands

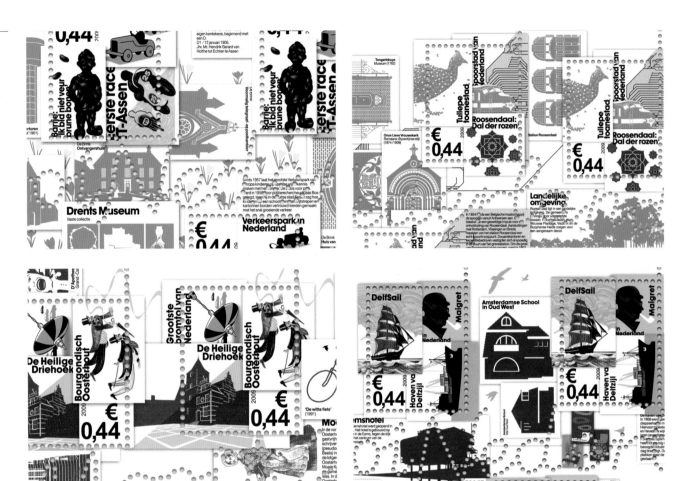

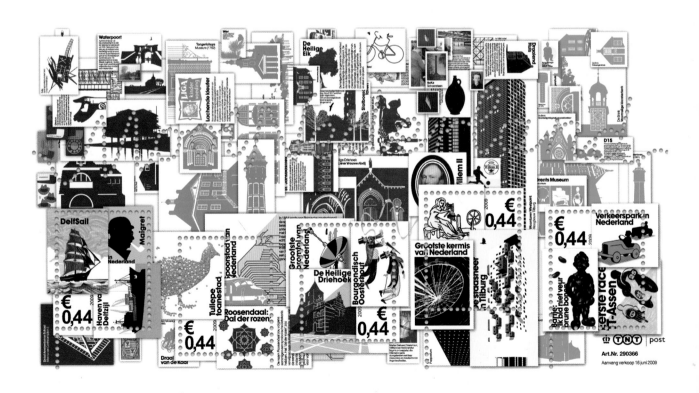

TITLE
Human Rights /Hionidis
for Amnesty International
COMPANY
Beetroot Design Group
CLIENT
Hionidis Men Fashion
ART DIRECTORS
Alexis Nikou
Vagelis Liakos
Yiannis Charalambopoulos
Michalis Rafail
Ilias Pantikakis
COUNTRY
Greece

# BRONZE
## MISCELLANEOUS PRINTED

**TITLE**
Transformation EMEX'09
**DESIGNER**
Viola Zimmermann
**CLIENT**
Buchbinderei Burckhardt AG
Sihl + Eika AG
Sonderergger AG
**COUNTRY**
Switzerland

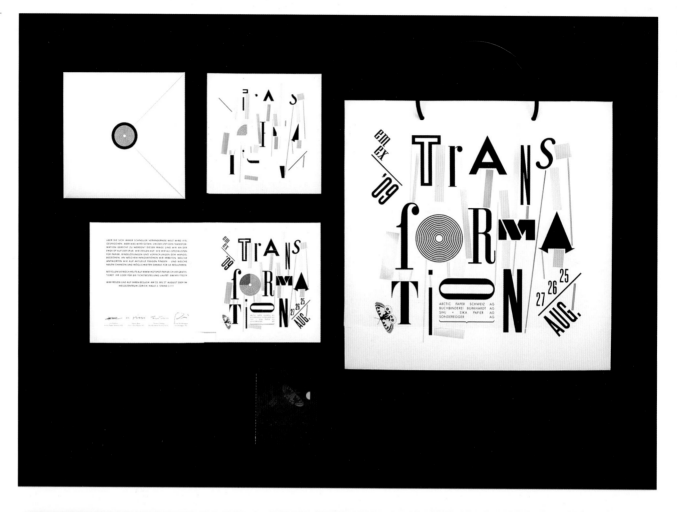

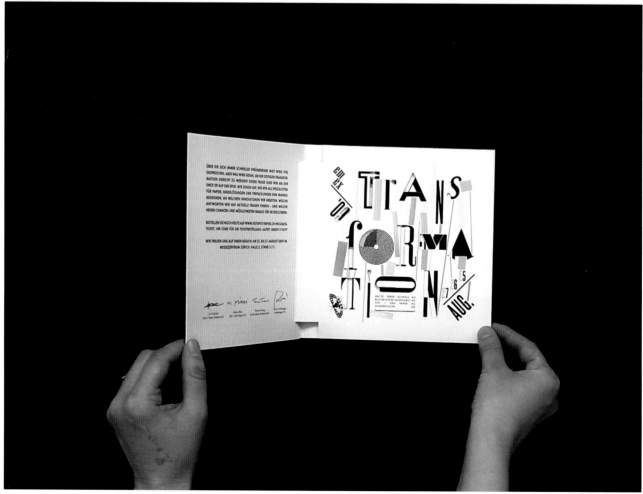

**TITLE**
Trool card game
**COMPANY**
Studio Kmzero
**CLIENT**
Istituto degli Innocenti /
Fondazione Sistema Toscana
**URL**
www.trool.it
**COUNTRY**
Italy

**TITLE**
Connected Women
**COMPANY**
Iola
**CLIENT**
PwC - Pricewaterhouse
Coopers Luxembourg
**COUNTRY**
Luxembourg

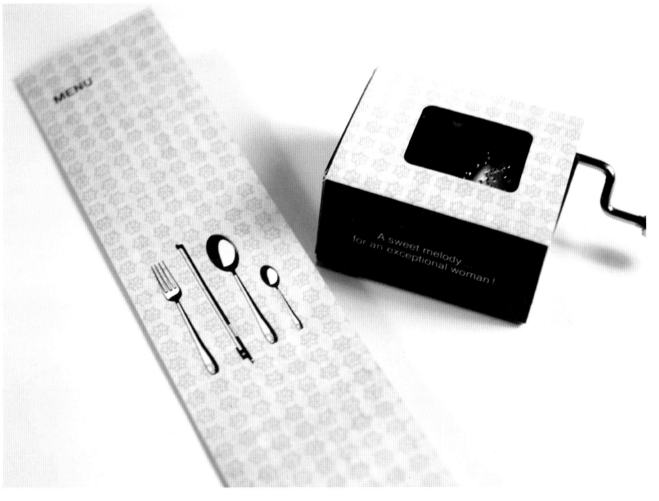

**TITLE**
Karim Rashid Lecture
**COMPANY**
bauer konzept & gestaltung
gmbh
**CLIENT**
Vienna University of Applied Arts
**COUNTRY**
Austria

**TITLE**
part of the art wrapping paper
**COMPANY**
traunig wurzinger gnbr
**CLIENT**
part of the art
**COUNTRY**
Austria

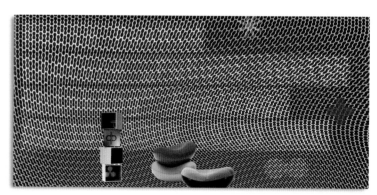

**TITLE**
Pairs Game
**COMPANY**
Paarpiloten
**CLIENT**
EDG Dortmund
**COUNTRY**
Germany

**TITLE**
La Poésie / Nuit
**COMPANY**
Tom Henni
**CLIENT**
Festival La Poésie / Nuit
**COUNTRY**
France

# 2010 | Gert Dumbar
## 2009 | Adrian Frutiger
## 2008 | Javier Mariscal
## 2007 | Erik Spiekermann

In their aim to properly acknowledge, honour and award people who invest their passion in design, the ED-Awards have created the European Designers Hall of Fame. Every year representatives from the fourteen partner design magazines come up with a list of nominees of people whose presence and exceptional work has inspired their peers as well as educated the public in regards to communication design in Europe. The community of European designers are then called to vote one out of these nominees. The winner of this process is the person who is inducted in the ED-Hall of fame every year.

# AGENCY OF
# THE YEAR

**COMPANY**
Lava
**COUNTRY**
The Netherlands

To determine the "European Design Agency of the year" a point system
has been developed. For each silver prize an agency wins, it receives
points equal to the number of submissions in that specific category. For
each gold prize, the points are equivalent to the numbers of submissions
in the category multiplied by three. All participating designeers/studios
are eligible for this distinction.

**TITLE**
Letterlab
**COMPANY**
Strange Attractors Design
**CLIENTS**
Graphic Design Museum,
Breda, The Netherlands
**DESIGNERS**
Ryan Pescatore Frisk,
Catelijne Van Middelkoop
**COPY WRITER**
Marieke Van Oudheusden
**EDITORS**
Ryan Pescatore Frisk,
Catelijne Van Middelkoop
**URL**
www.letterlab.com
**COUNTRY**
The Netherlands

This is the piece of work that, according to the jury, promotes design
best, within the wider public. All work submitted is automatically eligible for the Jury Prize, regardless of whether it is successful in any of the
main categories.

**TITLE**
Building for the 2000-Watt
Society: The State of Affairs
**COMPANY**
Raffinrie AG
**CLIENT**
City of Zurich
**DESIGNERS**
Simon Fuhrimann
Helen Pombo
**EDITORS**
Daniel Kurz
Karin Vasella-Kuhn
Anna Blattert
Tanja Reimer
Paul Knsel
**EXHIBITION CURATORS**
Karin Vasella-Kuhn
Daniel Kurz
**BUILT-UP
TECHNIQUE**
Holzer Kobler Architekturen
**COUNTRY**
Switzerland

This award recognizes the most exceptional piece of design in Europe during the previous year. The selection is made among all the category gold award winners. With the exception of winners coming from the self initiated projects, the self-promotional categories and the student projects, all other gold winners are elligible for this prize.

# INDEX

**G:** Gold, **S:** Silver, **B:** Bronze, **F:** Finalist

# CREDITS

**European Design Ltd**
Sokratous 157
176 73 Kallithea
Athens
Greece
**T** +30 210 9593033
**F** +30 210 9523607
info@europeandesign.org
www. europeandesign.org

**ISBN** 978-960-98284-2-0

Texts by Silvia Sfligiotti

Edited by Penny Analytis

Layout and design by busybuilding

www.europeandesign.org

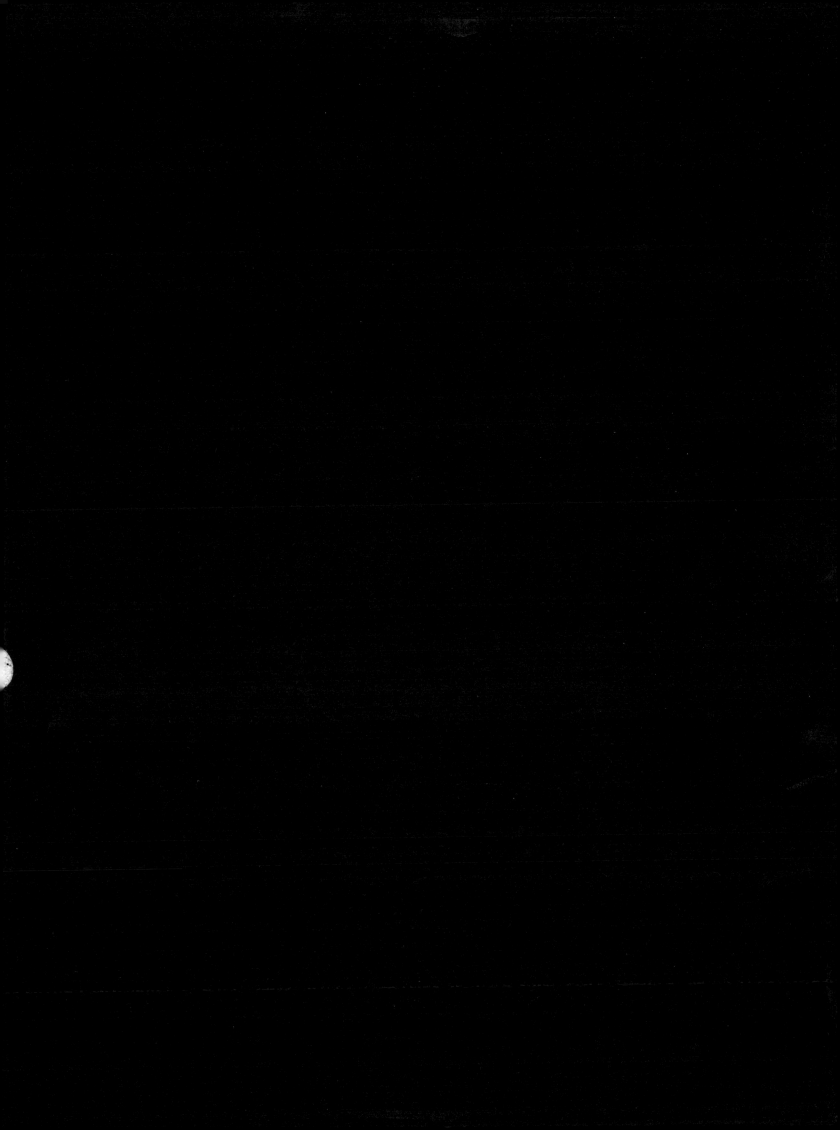